MW00713190

Cpl. William M. (Billy) Howard, United States Marine Corps, Fallujah, Iraq
– Submitted by his father and mother, David and Markie Howard.

With deep gratitude, this book is dedicated to the men and women of The United States Armed Forces, who provide us the freedom to enjoy Saturdays in the fall.

Tales of the Tide

## JARROD'S DEDICATION

To my mom, Jeannie Long Bazemore, and the
memory of my dad, Harvey Franklin Bazemore, Jr.,
my favorite Auburn fan.

## CLINT'S DEDICATION

To my wife, Anne, my greatest Bama story.
And to Coach Sammy Dunn, the love and respect
your players and fans have for you rivals that
of Coach Bryant.

TALES OF THE TIDE©
A BOOK BY ALABAMA FANS ... FOR ALABAMA FANS

Clint Lovette • Jarrod Bazemore
of
Lovette & Bazemore, LLC

Published by:

FANtastic Memories, LLC
P. O. Box 660582
Birmingham, AL 35266
www.FMbooks.net • info@FMbooks.net

All rights reserved. No part of this publication may be reproduced, stored in a retrieval system, or transmitted, in any form or by any means, electronic, mechanical, photocopying, recording, or otherwise, without prior written permission of the publisher except for the inclusion of brief quotations for review.

FANtastic Memories, LLC and Lovette & Bazemore, LLC have not made any attempt, and do not intend for this book, to insult or defame any person, team, entity, etc. Each submitting author has represented and warranted to FANtastic Memories, LLC that the material is original with the author; that the author has the exclusive right to grant all rights in the material; and that the author has the exclusive rights in the title of the material and in its use in connection with the material.

Edited by Carol Muse Evans.

Cover and Design by Atticus Communications, LLC

ISBN: 0-9740245-1-1

First Printing: September 2004

Copyright © 2001-2004 • FANtastic Memories, LLC

Printed in U.S.A.

# TALES OF THE TIDE

### A BOOK BY ALABAMA FANS…
### FOR ALABAMA FANS

Clint Lovette • Jarrod Bazemore

First Edition

Lee Roy Jordan and grandchildren

# FOREWORD

Behind every great program are great fans. No statement could be more true, and with respect to the University of Alabama, its fans are not merely a part of the storied tradition, they are the backbone. And the time has come for them to be properly recognized.

Rest assured, this book does just that.

When first approached about contributing to this work, though honored, I nevertheless withheld my assistance until I had the opportunity to evaluate the quality of the book's content. Since this book focuses on The University's most valuable asset, the fans, I had to ensure it was of the highest quality – anything less would be unacceptable. After reading the manuscript from cover to cover, I was immediately convinced that this book's goals have been fully achieved, and after reading it, you too will agree. Tales of the Tide is truly a book "by the fans and for the fans."

As you will see, this book is more than a compilation of great stories. Rather, on each of the pages, you will find treasured pieces of people's lives – lives which form part of something much larger than themselves – lives which make up the greatest tradition in the world, The University of Alabama.

While reading the manuscript, I thought about the many victories and championships we experienced during my playing career. I thought about Coach Bryant, my teammates, and the countless lessons I learned on the field of play. I also reflected on my undying devotion and love for The University, which continues though my playing days have long since passed. You see, I was an Alabama football player for only four years, but I have been a devout fan my entire life.

I have heard the old adage that every fan has a great story to tell. Allow me to share a few of mine.

I grew up in Excel, Alabama and was fortunate enough to be recruited by The University of Alabama. In fact, Assistant Coach Gene Stallings came to many of my high school games. Of course, I will never forget the first time I met Coach Bryant during a recruiting visit my senior year. When I arrived at Coach's office, he asked me to have a seat on his couch. Coach Bryant was already an intimidating person, and I cannot articulate the feeling of awe I had during our conversation as I sank down in the couch while looking up at the towering figure seated behind the desk. I was amazed at how much Coach Bryant already knew about me, both on and off the field. Needless to say, he was always prepared, a virtue he persistently endeavored to instill in his players. It was there in his office that Coach Bryant said he wanted me to become part of the Alabama Family, and with hard work and dedication, we could do great things. Indeed, we did.

We won the National Championship in 1961 and enjoyed a 29-2-2 record during my playing tenure. During these years, I had the honor of playing alongside great men like Pat Trammell, Billy Neighbors, Benny Nelson, Charlie Pell, Darwin Holt, Bill Battle, Joe Namath, Butch Wilson and many more. And we were taught by the greatest professor of all, Coach Bryant.

Coach Bryant was the greatest motivator this world has ever seen. Coach was not so much concerned with one player being better than another – it was more important to him that a player simply become the very best he could be, both on and off the field. Coach knew precisely when a player needed a kick in the butt or a pat on the back. At practice during the week before a big game, Coach was known for calling you aside, putting his arm around you, and telling you how he and the rest of the team were depending on you to have a big game and lead Alabama onto victory. After times like those, Saturday afternoon could not come quickly enough.

Of all the great games of which I was a part, the 1960 Georgia Tech game in Atlanta is among my favorites. We had played terribly during the entire first half, and as we sat in the locker room at halftime, we anticipated the very worst when Coach Bryant walked in. Actually, before Coach arrived, we were too scared to even take off our helmets out of fear of what might soon fly across the room. We just knew he was infuriated with our play even though the lack of execution was not for want of effort. Amazingly, Coach Bryant calmly walked in, and with his encouraging voice said, "Boys, we got 'em right where we want 'em. We're playing hard. We're gonna make some changes and win this game." And we did just that. As time expired, we kicked a field goal to win 16-15. You see, Coach knew our spirits were down, and instead of chewing us out about missed opportunities, he knew the exact words to say to get us to execute on the field.

When Jarrod and Clint approached me about writing this foreword, I not only remembered my experiences as a player, but I also reflected on my life as a fan. My best memories of The University are not of games on the field but rather the relationships built during my time there. I met my wife,

Biddie Banks, at The Capstone, and we have been married for 40 years. Actually, we were married by then-Alabama President Dr. Frank Rose, and we were honored by Coach and Mrs. Bryant's attendance at our wedding. Like many Alabama fans, Biddie Banks and I paid tribute to Coach Bryant by naming our son Christopher Bryant, and out of admiration for Pat Trammel, the gutsiest player I have ever known, we named an older son Patrick Lee.

As I stated before, my life has been molded by my time associated with The University, but none of that would have been possible without the foundation upon which it is all built – the fans. And that is why I love this book.

As you read Tales of the Tide, I hope you will literally feel the same enthusiasm and passion as I did, bringing you to one underlying truth. This is not just a publication of fans' stories, it is the lifeblood of Alabama, and I am proud to say my greatest honor is simply being one of you – an Alabama fan.

Lee Roy Jordan
Bama Fan

Bryant-Denny Stadium

Jarrod Bazemore and Clint Lovette

# TABLE OF CONTENTS

FOREWORD . . . . . . . . . . . . . . . . . . . . . . . . . . . . . . . . . . . . . . . . . . . . . . .vii

THIS IS ALABAMA . . . . . . . . . . . . . . . . . . . . . . . . . . . . . . . . . . . . . . .1

SLEEPING WITH THE ENEMY . . . . . . . . . . . . . . . . . . . . . . . . . . . . .7

ARE YOU KIN TO THAT KICKER? . . . . . . . . . . . . . . . . . . . . . . . . .11

HEART AND SOUL . . . . . . . . . . . . . . . . . . . . . . . . . . . . . . . . . . . . . . .17

WE SPOOKED OL' STEVE . . . . . . . . . . . . . . . . . . . . . . . . . . . . . . . . .21

CHRISTMAS 1980, 315, AND THE
RICHEST TRADITION IN COLLEGE FOOTBALL . . . . . . . . . . . . . . .25

CONVERSION . . . . . . . . . . . . . . . . . . . . . . . . . . . . . . . . . . . . . . . . . . .29

CURSE OF THE BAMBINO? . . . . . . . . . . . . . . . . . . . . . . . . . . . . . .37

THAT'S MY BOY . . . . . . . . . . . . . . . . . . . . . . . . . . . . . . . . . . . . . . . . .43

INCOMING! . . . . . . . . . . . . . . . . . . . . . . . . . . . . . . . . . . . . . . . . . . . .49

TWISTS OF FATE . . . . . . . . . . . . . . . . . . . . . . . . . . . . . . . . . . . . . . . .53

BEAR'S BUG . . . . . . . . . . . . . . . . . . . . . . . . . . . . . . . . . . . . . . . . . . . .59

FIRST GENERATION GRADUATE . . . . . . . . . . . . . . . . . . . . . . . . . .63

LARGER THAN LIFE . . . . . . . . . . . . . . . . . . . . . . . . . . . . . . . . . . . . . .67

SMELLS LIKE TEAM SPIRIT . . . . . . . . . . . . . . . . . . . . . . . . . . . . . . . .71

FAMILY TRADITION . . . . . . . . . . . . . . . . . . . . . . . . . . . . . . . . . . . . .77

SOME THINGS NEVER CHANGE . . . . . . . . . . . . . . . . . . . . . . . . . .80

A TALE OF TWO UNCLES . . . . . . . . . . . . . . . . . . . . . . . . . . . . . . . .83

VICTORY ON THE PLAINS . . . . . . . . . . . . . . . . . . . . . . . . . . . . . . . .89

HEY BEAR, LOOK AT ME! . . . . . . . . . . . . . . . . . . . . . . . . . . . . . . . .93

WILL I EVER MEET THE BEAR? . . . . . . . . . . . . . . . . . . . . . . . . . . . .97

TALES FROM THE TRUNK . . . . . . . . . . . . . . . . . . . . . . . . . . . . . . . . . . .103

GROWING UP WITH THE TIDE . . . . . . . . . . . . . . . . . . . . . . . . . . . . .107

THE BAMA KING . . . . . . . . . . . . . . . . . . . . . . . . . . . . . . . . . . . . . . . . .111

OH HAPPY DAY! . . . . . . . . . . . . . . . . . . . . . . . . . . . . . . . . . . . . . . . . .115

SHORTY PRICE . . . . . . . . . . . . . . . . . . . . . . . . . . . . . . . . . . . . . . . . . . .119

A PRAYER FOR THE TIDE . . . . . . . . . . . . . . . . . . . . . . . . . . . . . . . . . .121

THE GIFT OF A HAT . . . . . . . . . . . . . . . . . . . . . . . . . . . . . . . . . . . . . .125

THAT WAS KICKOFF . . . . . . . . . . . . . . . . . . . . . . . . . . . . . . . . . . . . . .129

"THIS IS FOR YOU DADDY..." . . . . . . . . . . . . . . . . . . . . . . . . . . . . .133

J.R.² . . . . . . . . . . . . . . . . . . . . . . . . . . . . . . . . . . . . . . . . . . . . . . . . . . . . .137

RUBBING ELBOWS . . . . . . . . . . . . . . . . . . . . . . . . . . . . . . . . . . . . . . .145

PART OF THE GAME . . . . . . . . . . . . . . . . . . . . . . . . . . . . . . . . . . . . . .149

FINALLY SEEING IT IN PERSON . . . . . . . . . . . . . . . . . . . . . . . . . . . .153

SWAMP MEAT . . . . . . . . . . . . . . . . . . . . . . . . . . . . . . . . . . . . . . . . . . .155

TROPICAL DEPRESSION . . . . . . . . . . . . . . . . . . . . . . . . . . . . . . . . . .159

GLORIOUS HAPPY VALLEY . . . . . . . . . . . . . . . . . . . . . . . . . . . . . . .163

THE LUCK STOPS HERE . . . . . . . . . . . . . . . . . . . . . . . . . . . . . . . . . .165

THE MAN . . . . . . . . . . . . . . . . . . . . . . . . . . . . . . . . . . . . . . . . . . . . . . .167

MY BEAR . . . . . . . . . . . . . . . . . . . . . . . . . . . . . . . . . . . . . . . . . . . . . . . .171

17 TO 16 IS NO MORE . . . . . . . . . . . . . . . . . . . . . . . . . . . . . . . . . . . .174

A "BIG EASY" WIN . . . . . . . . . . . . . . . . . . . . . . . . . . . . . . . . . . . . . . .177

STUDENT LIFE ON THE RUN . . . . . . . . . . . . . . . . . . . . . . . . . . . . .187

BUZZER BEATER . . . . . . . . . . . . . . . . . . . . . . . . . . . . . . . . . . . . . . . . .191

LET'S PUT IT IN PERSPECTIVE . . . . . . . . . . . . . . . . . . . . . . . . . . . .195

BRUSH WITH GREATNESS . . . . . . . . . . . . . . . . . . . . . . . . . . . . . . . .197

ALABAMA FUTEBOL . . . . . . . . . . . . . . . . . . . . . . . . . . . . . . . . . . . . .199

THE TIDE THAT BINDS . . . . . . . . . . . . . . . . . . . . . . . . . . . . . . . . .203

NO SADNESS IN MUDVILLE ON THIS BAMA DAY
ALABAMA 9 – SOUTHERN CALIFORNIA 8 . . . . . . . . . . . . . . . . . .207

TAILGATING HOSPITALITY . . . . . . . . . . . . . . . . . . . . . . . . . . . . . . .211

ON THE ROAD AGAIN . . . . . . . . . . . . . . . . . . . . . . . . . . . . . . . . . .213

THE GOAL-LINE ANNIVERSARY . . . . . . . . . . . . . . . . . . . . . . . . . . .219

THE WINNING TICKET . . . . . . . . . . . . . . . . . . . . . . . . . . . . . . . . . .223

A BAMA BIRTHDAY . . . . . . . . . . . . . . . . . . . . . . . . . . . . . . . . . . . . .225

BIG AL AND THE BARBEQUE GALS . . . . . . . . . . . . . . . . . . . . . . . .227

WATCHING MY COUSIN IN IRON BOWL 1971 . . . . . . . . . . . . . .230

A LAWSON FAMILY ROADTRIP . . . . . . . . . . . . . . . . . . . . . . . . . . .233

OVERTIME REBIRTH . . . . . . . . . . . . . . . . . . . . . . . . . . . . . . . . . . . .239

A DATE TO REMEMBER . . . . . . . . . . . . . . . . . . . . . . . . . . . . . . . . .243

NAMESAKES AND NEW ORLEANS ALABAMA LEGACIES . . . . . . .247

MORE TO COME. . . . . . . . . . . . . . . . . . . . . . . . . . . . . . . . . . . . . . .253


ABOUT THE AUTHORS . . . . . . . . . . . . . . . . . . . . . . . . . . . . . . . . .257

THANK YOU . . . . . . . . . . . . . . . . . . . . . . . . . . . . . . . . . . . . . . . . . .258

TALES OF THE TIDE© SUPPORTERS . . . . . . . . . . . . . . . . . . . . . . .259

AUTHOR INDEX . . . . . . . . . . . . . . . . . . . . . . . . . . . . . . . . . . . . . .274

FUTURE BOOK INFORMATION . . . . . . . . . . . . . . . . . . . . . . . . . .275

QUICK ORDER FORM . . . . . . . . . . . . . . . . . . . . . . . . . . . . . . . . . .276

Anne and Clint Lovette

*"I had found a place that didn't change for the sake of change but instead embraced the lessons that success and tradition teach us and pass those lessons down to the people that care about becoming part of something bigger than themselves."*

*– Clint Lovette*

# THIS IS ALABAMA...

I have to admit that when I approached Jarrod Bazemore (my brother-in-law) about doing this book, I felt like it might not be the greatest time in the world. While the University had just come off a great basketball season by reaching the Elite 8, I was concerned that due to the challenges faced by the football program over the last few years, we would not get the participation from Bama fans we needed to produce this book.

I have never been more proud to be proved so wrong.

This project began because an Auburn book was released in the fall of 2003. I picked up the book (keep your friends close and your enemies closer) long enough to "flip" the pages and get an idea of what it was all about. I have yet to read the book and have no future plans to waste an afternoon reading stories from Auburn fans whose greatest memories involve running to a corner and rolling trees with toilet paper… but I digress. As I was saying, this project began because I saw that book, loved the idea, and I began to think about how much better an Alabama book would be and how much I love hearing stories from other fans. I made contact with the publisher in December of 2003 and expressed my interest in heading up a similar project for Alabama. They agreed to let Jarrod and me head up the project, and we were both extremely excited about the prospect of gathering, compiling, and listening to stories from Bama fans who are as passionate about The University as we are. My concerns about the interest in this book were quashed the first week we got started.

Jarrod and I are not professional writers but rather both have full time careers, so we relied heavily on getting the word out about the book through friends, family, coworkers, and random people we would meet. The response was overwhelming, and I hope after you read this book, you will agree. I am now a bigger Alabama fan than I have ever been in my life and my respect for the tradition that has been built for more than 100 years at The University ranks close to my respect for the Armed Forces that have protected this great nation.

As we started this project, I knew I would need to share a few stories in the book, and I began to think about great moments and memories that I have about Alabama.

I started thinking about growing up in a house where my dad was a high school football coach and how many references on a weekly basis he would make to Alabama and Coach Bryant. He even ran the wishbone as his offense because that's what the successful Alabama teams of the 1970s were doing. My first memories of Alabama are the games my dad would take me to at Legion Field. We would always take the binoculars and get to the game early so we could see Coach Bryant lean against the goal post and watch his team prepare for battle. I still remember my dad pointing to Coach Bryant while I looked through the binoculars and saying, "When you grow up, if you have a positive impact on half as many lives as that man has, you will be a great success."

I then started thinking about my years at the Capstone getting my degree. I remember my first day of orientation. Our Avanti (orientation staff) counselor went around the room at Ten Hoor Hall and asked us why we decided to attend The University. About 70 percent of the people in the room responded because of the football team. I will never forget his response: "Don't ever let someone give you a hard time about attending college here because of the football team. I will promise you this, you came here because of the football team but you will leave here with an appreciation of what the Alabama tradition is all about, and that understanding will stay with you the rest of your life."

He was right. One of my first business classes at Alston Hall began with the professor playing a 30-minute video of Coach Bryant and the techniques he used with his assistant coaches… it was an Introduction to Management class. I knew I had found a home. I had found a place that didn't change for the sake of change but instead embraced the lessons that success and tradition teach us and pass those lessons down to the people that care about becoming part of something bigger than themselves.

I also felt at home when I went to the barber shop on 15th Street my freshman year, and as I sat in one of the three chairs, I heard "Have a seat Coach." Coach Stallings sat down next to me, and we began to talk about the season as if I was discussing it with my father. My piece of notebook paper that says, "To Clint, Haircut Buddies, Gene Stallings" still hangs in my office.

I thought about how studying and classes would end on Thursday, or no later than noon on Friday, during football season, and we would begin our pre-game "activities" on the Strip that evening. I was fortunate (I didn't always think so) to spend my last two years at Alabama in an apartment directly behind the Strip. To be exact, I could walk to Pepito's and Chang's restaurants in about five seconds. My roommate and I would sit out on the porch in front of our apartment late Friday evenings and early Saturday mornings and watch the Bama fans make their way to the Strip. We would of course encourage them on their way with a loud "Roll Tide." I can't tell you how many random conversations I had with fans strolling by our apartment and how many ended up in our living room sharing a beverage and telling stories about when they were down at the Capstone and how much they missed it. As I was rehashing these memories, I couldn't help but laugh about how many times we would walk to the Kwik Snak late Friday night (actually, I'm not sure it opened before midnight) and down a "Big Nasty." For those of you not fortunate enough to attend or visit The University while Kwik Snak was open, a "Big Nasty" is a plate of cheese tots covered with chili and topped with a fried egg. I have attempted to recreate this combination at multiple Waffle Houses throughout the state for nostalgic reasons, but there's nothing like the original.

Every time I go back to The University for a game, I walk down the Strip and remember when everything was not so nice. Though we all welcome the progress that has been and continues to be made to this area, I sure miss going to International Deli for a Reuben, the Ivory Tusk to see Mel and the Party Hats, and mooching off my girlfriend (and now wife) at Phi Mu formals at the Train Station, but thank goodness for the ever-present staples of the Houndstooth, The Booth, and Gallette's.

As I was going through old pictures, VCR tapes of past games, and memorabilia that would jog some great memories and experiences to share, I realized that there was one great experience that trumped all others.

This project.

This has by far been the best experience centered on the University of Alabama I have ever had. The stories in this book are a compilation of Bama fans' greatest and most personal memories, and as you read them, you begin to realize how much The University affects people's lives. All of the stories in this book are an extension of that person's personality, and you almost feel like you actually know them when you have read their stories. I have had the honor of listening to former players like Lee Roy Jordan, Steve Sloan and Mike Kennedy talk about their love for the fans, and reading stories from Chad Hopper make you want to find him at a game and hear him talk more about his wife (you'll understand after you read his story).

I have learned more about the tradition of Alabama by compiling these stories than I ever knew before. My hope is that one day you will be sitting at your tailgate before an Alabama game, remember one of the stories from this book and share it with another fan because that's what this book is all about – Alabama fans sharing their love for one simple and powerful thing…

The University of Alabama

Clint Lovette '98
Birmingham, Alabama

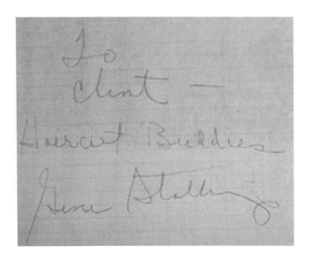

Chad & Brooke Hopper

*"People tell me that I should buy for our family vehicle a 'House Divided' car tag with one side Alabama and one side Auburn. I refuse because I will not allow anything Auburn on my automobile."*

*– Chad Hopper*

# SLEEPING
# WITH THE ENEMY

T he only good thing about Auburn University left it on June 10, 2000. That's right, I married an Auburn graduate. My wife, Brooke, received her Bachelor's degree in Elementary Education from Auburn and left The Plains on that date. And for all of her qualities that won my heart, such as her sweet southern charm and beautiful brown eyes, her one bad quality haunts me every fall.

You see, Brooke is not a typical female football fan. She is an Auburn football fanatic. We started dating during my last year as a student at Alabama, which was her last year at Auburn. Brooke has been known to cry after an Auburn loss to Alabama, then refuse to speak to me for days, as if I had something to do with the outcome of the game. No Alabama prints can be hung on our living room walls. On the rare occasion when she attends a Bama game with me (Auburn must be off, of course), she has to wear some sort of Auburn clothing. I am the President of the local Cherokee County Alabama Alumni Association, but I attend all of our banquets alone.

I am an Alabama football fanatic, season ticket holder, and I hate Auburn. No Auburn prints can be hung on our living room walls. People tell me that I should buy for our family vehicle a "House Divided" car tag with one side Alabama and one side Auburn. I refuse because I will not allow anything Auburn on my automobile. I cheer for any team that plays the

Tigers. Even if an Auburn win would help Bama in the SEC West standings, I cannot root for them. Brooke is an officer in the Cherokee County Auburn Club, yet she also attends all of her banquets alone.

As you can imagine, this makes for very interesting Iron Bowl games. We have attended every Alabama-Auburn contest together since 1999. The feeling on the Friday before the game is better than the feeling as a child on Christmas Eve. Brooke and I enjoy all of the pre-game festivities on Friday night because we are both still speaking to each other. On Saturday, we try to meet up with friends for tailgating. After that is the long walk to the stadium. When we reach the stadium, we go to our separate seats. She has to sit with her people, and I have to sit with mine. We honestly both still get chill bumps each time our respective teams run onto the field. After the game, one of us has to wait outside the stadium as the other cheers inside. The 2001 Iron Bowl was a great moment in recent Alabama history, and I stayed until the band had packed up and all of the players had left the field. Brooke, as did most of the Auburn faithful that day, left the game midway through the 3rd quarter. There is nothing as nice as seeing Tiger fans bail out of Jordan-Hare in the 3rd quarter of the biggest game of the season.

There is no hope for her conversion. She is the woman that I love more than life itself, and I truly feel sorry for her sometimes because she does not know what it is like to bleed crimson and white. She does not know, nor will she ever know, what it is like to cheer for a national championship team. She will never have the feeling of singing "Ramma Jamma" with 20,000 Bama fans at Neyland Stadium on the Third Saturday in October. Her idea of tradition involves lemonade, toilet paper, and an obscure small town pharmacy.

So, to all of the married folks who are equally yoked, remember to be thankful in your prayers. You can buy all of the Alabama memorabilia that you want. You can have your family's picture taken beside Denny Chimes after a big Bama win. You can enjoy ribs at Dreamland prior to the game, then sit with your spouse at an Iron Bowl. You have a lot for which to be thankful. And while saying your prayers, please add something about me at the end.

Pray for my future children.


Chad A. Hopper '00
Centre, AL

Tailgating in '89
L-R: Bob Tiffin, Kelly Moore, Van Tiffin, Tim Tiffin,
Shanna Moore – Middle Seated: Greta Stockton

*"I turned to my wife and said, 'That will be a kick Bama fans will never forget!' As the crowd rushed the field (something I had never seen a Bama crowd do before) I was overwhelmed with emotion. My son, the young boy that had kicked field goals six days a week in a field in Red Bay, Alabama, was being carried off the field by his Crimson teammates."*

*– Bob Tiffin*

---  𝒜  ---

# ARE YOU KIN TO THAT KICKER?

Since 1972, my motor home business has taken me all over the country, and I have had the opportunity to meet some wonderful people. Even to this day, almost 20 years later, when people find out I am from Alabama and my last name is Tiffin, they ask the inevitable question: Are you kin to that kicker?

I grew up as an Alabama fan, and I still remember how excited my family was when we found out that Coach Bryant was coming home to Alabama to lead our young men on the football field. In our local alumni meeting where Coach Bryant came to speak before the first season, he told us that he couldn't make any promises about the first season as he would be "putting his system in place and grooming the boys to win," but he promised from his second season on, the team's primary goal every year would be to beat Auburn. As I recall, he kept his promise, and we almost never lost to Auburn during his reign.

My kids obviously grew up Bama fans, and my wife and I always dreamed of our sons attending our beloved University or maybe even having the chance to play for the Bear. In 1980, Van started to get serious about sports and was especially drawn towards football. He was not the largest kid in school, so I sent him to Ft. Lauderdale that summer to a kicking camp. He had a gift for kicking and worked hard as he went through his high school career. He would go out to a field every afternoon and kick for a few hours, and I can remember spending at least a couple days a week shagging balls for him. He kept dreaming and working towards his goal of playing for the Tide, and his hard work paid off as Alabama began recruiting him. As with most kickers back then, Van was recruited by the Tide but was not given a scholarship right off the bat. He would have to go to Tuscaloosa and try out for the team.

In the fall of 1983, Van went to the University of Alabama and attempted to work his way onto the team and don a crimson jersey on Saturdays for the Tide. Although Coach Bryant was no longer with us, he had left his mark on the program and our family, and we were all excited that Coach Perkins had taken the torch to continue the tradition. I was extremely nervous for Van, and we spoke almost every day during August as he tried to impress the coaching staff and make the team. He was amazed at the level of talent that came to The University. I remember him calling me and talking about this linebacker they called "Biscuit." He told me there was no one in college fast enough to block him and that he was glad he was a kicker after he saw how hard this guy hit people. There were players who could have accepted scholarships at Division I schools, but they chose to walk on at Bama so they could play for the Tide. Everyday, Van would tell me he didn't think he was as good as the other kickers, but in the same breath, he would say he got more reps in front of the coaches that day. I kept telling him to work hard like he was back in Red Bay kicking in the field and things would work out. On September 6th, Van called us on his birthday, and he was extremely excited because Coach Perkins had just paid him a visit to tell him he had made the team and that he would be starting against Georgia Tech that Saturday. What a birthday present! He was 2 for 3 against Georgia Tech that Saturday, and he went on to lead the team in scoring his freshman year. In 1977, we went to our first Iron Bowl in our motor home.

Prior to that point, I had always worked the falls ginning cotton and was unable to make the games, but we always listened on the radio or watched on TV. At that game in '77, I counted 35 motor homes at the Iron Bowl. In 2002, there was a reported 600 motor homes in attendance. I guess the idea caught on. I won't spend 40 pages telling you about our friendships and memories we have from attending Bama games in our motor home, but I can tell you that Van's time at Bama was the most exciting time to tailgate for us. The most obvious memory is the Iron Bowl of 1985.

We were all excited about the 1985 Iron Bowl as both teams had great athletes, and the match up would prove to be a great battle. My parents went down with us for the game, and I will never forget that they dressed up for Bama games like they were heading to church. My father had on his best suit, and my mother wore her best dress. They were going to go see their grandson play for the Tide, and they would not have dressed any other way. On our way to our seats, we passed Van's future father-in-law, Mitchell Self, and his good friend Roy Horton. Roy was a huge Auburn fan, and as we passed by their seats, he asked my dad, "How do you feel about the game Mr. Tiffin?" My father responded very simply, "I didn't come to the game to get beat by Auburn." I had a good feeling as we walked to our seats.

All Alabama fans remember how that game went and what a great struggle it was for both teams, but the last minute of that game defined the personality of Alabama. When we got the ball back with 57 seconds, I knew the game might come down to a kick from Van. I could only just sit there and hope it would come to that. When Richardson drug the Auburn defender out of bounds, I remember my wife put her head in her hands because she was too afraid to watch her son be put in such a stressful situation. As Van ran onto the field with his teammates, my wife had her eyes closed, and my parents had actually sat down. None of them could bear to watch. There was no time to even think about the situation, and before I knew it, Van had kicked the ball toward the uprights. When he kicked it, I knew he had hit it well, but from 60 rows up, I couldn't tell if it was good. I had to look for the officials' signal. It wasn't just good…it was great! I turned to my wife and said, "That will be a kick Bama fans will never forget!" As the crowd rushed the field (something I had never seen a Bama crowd do before), I was overwhelmed with emotion. My son, the young boy that had kicked field goals six days a week in a field in Red Bay, Alabama, was being carried off the field by his teammates.

I would later hear from our friends, who were listening on the radio that night, about the great call from Paul Kennedy and Doug Layton:

Kennedy: "15 seconds to go, again from the 46…Bell in motion…Shula keeping a back in for protection. Looks… steps… looking… looking… dumping… open Richardson… head to the boundary Greg… head to the boundary… get out of bounds! He does! 35 yard line… 6 seconds to go… let's bring on the field goal unit!"

Layton: "Got to, there's only time for one more play. The ball's at the Auburn 36, so it's gonna be about a 52-yard attempt. A 52-yard attempt will be it for Van Tiffin."

Kennedy: "This would win the game. A 52-yard try. The clock will not start till the ball is snapped. There is the snap…the kick…it is in the air…IT HAS DISTANCE…IT'S GOOD! IT'S GOOD!

Layton: "It's Good."

Kennedy: "It's Good."

Layton: "It's Good."

Kennedy: "It's Good."

Layton: "Van Tiffin has won the ball game!"

Kennedy: "Alabama has beaten Auburn. Van Tiffin has kicked a 52-yard field goal! And the state of Alabama is CRIMSON!"

It almost makes me wish I had heard it on the radio.

We went back to the motor home in elation and began to cook the traditional post game meal. What seemed like an endless stream of Bama fans came by and congratulated us on Van's kick. It was then that I was most proud of Van, not because the fans were recognizing us for our son's accomplishment, but because we were watching the replay that was being shown on ABC every 30 minutes when the phrase "the kick" would be coined. I was so proud of the kick that Van made under pressure, but I was even more proud of the interview that Van did after the game with the sideline reporter, Tim Brandt, and the comments he made about his team. My boy had become a man in one short November afternoon.

Now, as I watch Van's son (Leigh Tiffin) kick as a young member of his high school team, I can only hope that one day he will have the opportunity to follow in his father's footsteps.

Roll Tide!

Bob Tiffin
Red Bay, Alabama

Steve Sloan, Alabama Quarterback 1963-65

*"To this day, Alabama fans surprise me with their level of commitment to the program and to the tradition that has been built. I still get something in the mail once a week from an Alabama fan asking for an autograph, and I think how humbled and honored I am to have been part of a program where the fans care so much and truly bleed Crimson."*

*– Steve Sloan - Alabama QB 1963-65*

# HEART AND SOUL

To me, the grass roots Alabama fan is the heart and soul of what Alabama is all about. In my years at Alabama, I was blessed to be surrounded by some of the greatest fans in the world, and I am still close to many of them.

I grew up in Cleveland, Tennessee, and I actually pulled for UT and Georgia Tech as a young fan, but all of that would change when I went to the Capstone in 1963. I chose Alabama because of the program Coach Bryant had built and the effort his excellent staff put into recruiting me. I, however, was not prepared for the level of attention being a quarterback at Alabama can bring.

I will never forget our first team meeting with Coach Bryant. There were about 60 freshmen all gathered in the room waiting for him to speak. While we were waiting, you could look around the room and know that many of those players would not make it under Coach Bryant. It was very difficult to even make the team, much less start, and Coach Bryant and his staff worked us harder than I have ever been worked in my life. Coach Bryant was larger than life and commanded respect like a Czar. The program was so structured and the assistants were so loyal to Coach Bryant and to that structure, you knew some of those guys were not going to make it. But I had come to Alabama to get a degree and play ball for The University, and failing to do either was not an option.

One thing that amazed me about Alabama fans is that they exemplified the same level of commitment that Coach Bryant demanded from his players and coaches. A great example of this is when Coach Bryant would get all of the quarterbacks together before the game and take a "stroll" around the campus right before leaving for the stadium. The number of fans that would follow us during our "stroll" was unbelievable, and I really believe Alabama football was a way for those fans to escape from some of the tough economic times during the 60s. It was almost like you would make a heart-to-heart connection with fans and carry an extra burden to win for the fans who would come out every Saturday to live and die with the Tide.

To this day, Alabama fans surprise me with their level of commitment to the program and to the tradition that has been built. I still get something in the mail once a week from an Alabama fan asking for an autograph, and I think how humbled and honored I am to have been part of a program where the fans care so much and truly bleed crimson.

The National Championship in 1965 brings back great memories of the fans. We were headed to the Orange Bowl for the second straight year to play Nebraska for what would essentially become the national championship game for us. There was a pretty interesting turn of events to get us to that point. We were actually ranked #4 in the polls going into that week, but after losses from #1 Michigan State to UCLA and #2 Arkansas to LSU, we had catapulted into the #1 ranking before the Orange Bowl kicked off, and the only thing standing in our way of a national title were the #3-ranked Cornhuskers.

The Alabama fans were once again showing their passion by taking over the city of Miami for the entire week. We had a pep rally in the hotel a day before the game, and even after being at Alabama for a few years, I was still amazed at the number of people in attendance and the spirit they brought with them. The strategy for the game was laid out by Coach

Bryant in a peculiar way. You see, the team was taking a boat ride in a typical bowl week type activity, when Coach Bryant pulled me to the side and said, "I want you to throw the ball anytime... short yardage, long yardage, first downs and even when we are backed up." I was shocked at first because that was never part of our plan, mainly because we could stop just about anyone on defense. However, as I thought about it, I think Coach Bryant really respected Nebraska's offense, and he felt like we might have to put some points on the board to win... and he was right.

Coach Bryant pulled out all of the stops that game which included 3 on-side kicks. During the end of the second quarter, Coach Bryant sent in a second-string guard with a message for me, "Coach Bryant said to tell you that you don't HAVE to throw it every down!" We didn't throw it as much in the second half because I had broken my ribs near the end of the first, but Coach's plan worked, and we won the game (39-28) and the national championship. That whole week was a great experience for me, and I will never forget the pride on the fans' faces after the game.

As a fan of the program and an obvious fan of Coach Bryant, I was deeply saddened when he passed away. I was able to attend his funeral and the overwhelming response of the fans and the mourning that took place throughout the state (and really the country) was astonishing. I remember feeling really disappointed that Coach did not get some time to do the things you should enjoy in retirement. He gave so much to The University, and I wish he could have enjoyed his friends and family away from the program for at least a few more years.

If there is one person that has ever embodied the true heart and soul of an Alabama fan, it would be Tony Brandino. Tony means so much to all of the coaches, players and fans of the program. His story is well chronicled about how he went to 500 straight Bama games over a course of 43 years. He has all kinds of stories to tell, but I just remember what he and his brother meant to me as a player. Tony was like another coach on the staff, and for those of you that have played sports, you know how influential and meaningful a relationship that can be. It was like he represented all Alabama fans, and he was able to attend every game for every Alabama fan.

Tony's twin brother passed away while I was at Alabama, and I remember Coach Bailey coming to me one day and saying that Tony had requested that I be a pall bearer in the funeral. I was truly honored to do that for Tony. I have never known someone that was so dedicated to something that it truly was a part of his soul. I guess that's what being a Bama fan is all about.

Steve Sloan
Alabama QB 1963-65
All American, National Champion
Assistant Coach 1968-70
Athletic Director 1987-89
Fan

# WE SPOOKED OL' STEVE

The day we tricked Steve Sloan into staying with the Crimson Tide program as quarterbacks coach and offensive coordinator ranks up there with the best. It happened during the 1960s; just after his playing career ended. We were beating up on opponents and other programs were trying to hire our assistant coaches. Tennessee made a hard run at Sloan, a native of that state, and he was thinking about moving to Knoxville.

As Sloan was weighing the pros and cons of that move, he had a dream in which he was walking down Gay Street in Knoxville. He told some of the other assistant coaches about it. He said everybody he saw was faceless, except for one person. That singular person with a face was Tony Brandino. Well, Sloan was always an emotional guy, as well as a highly spiritual person, and he was confused. Also, I'm sure he was searching for a hidden meaning.

The day he told the others about the dream, Sam Bailey, an assistant coach who would become associate athletic director, telephoned me. I got a message instructing me to call (radio announcer) Doug Layton or Sam Bailey as soon as possible. I tried to reach Doug and failed. After a couple of tries, I got in touch with Sam at the athletic department. Bailey told me about Sloan's dream and suggested it might be a good time for me to talk to him. In other words, he thought that might make the dream seem real.

I reached Sloan the next morning. I said, "Steve, I understand you're thinking about going to Tennessee and, for the life of me, I can't understand why. You're an Alabama guy. I don't think you'll fit in up there."

There was a long pause. Then Sloan responded in an excitable voice. He said, "Tony, I don't believe this is happening because…" He told me about the dream. I acted surprised and suggested the Good Lord was sending him a message. Then he said, "I can tell you right now I'm not going up there."

-Excerpt from FANtastic by Tony Brandino

Tony Brandino, halfway to #500.

Coach Bryant, Peggy Poore, Ruth Long Savage (Jarrod's grand-mother), Jarrod Bazemore (age 2) and Jeannie Bazemore (Jarrod's mom) in 1975 at Cherokee County Bank where Jarrod's dad and grandmother worked

*"Though he was a staunch Auburn fan, I will always appreciate my dad putting me on his shoulders so that I could observe this momentous occasion, and will forever be grateful for him enduring my constant desire to talk about this game whenever football was discussed. Put simply, it was # 315, and I was there."*

*– Jarrod Bazemore*

—— 𝒜 ——

# CHRISTMAS 1980, 315, AND THE RICHEST TRADITION IN COLLEGE FOOTBALL

For all practical purposes, I grew up in an Auburn family, but much to the chagrin of my dad, I discovered early in my childhood that I bleed crimson and white. It was Christmas Eve, 1980, at my grandparents' home in Centre, Alabama, when I, though destined to be an Auburn Tiger, received as a gift a long sleeved crimson t-shirt which read, "Alabama 1979 National Champions #1."

I cannot remember who gave me this shirt, but I can certainly attest to the manner in which it changed my perceived future and positively impacted my life. Upon opening the gift, I asked my dad what did "#1" mean, to which he responded that Alabama was the best team in the country the previous year. From that moment forward, my fate was sealed. I was "Bama Bound" in the truest sense of the words, which was certainly demonstrated later that night when I, for lack of a better phrase, pitched a fit upon receiving an Auburn jacket from my aunt and uncle.

My earliest memory of attending an Alabama game was November 28, 1981. Though some may not immediately recognize the significance of this date, everyone within the boundaries of our great state, as well as college football fans throughout the country, certainly recognizes the significance of the number "315." I attended this game with my dad and two grandfathers, and despite the fact that we may have cheered for different teams, I will always cherish the fact that I had the opportunity to be in their company on such a special occasion. To witness Coach Bryant become the winningest coach in college football history was truly an honor, and I cannot begin to articulate what it meant to see this achievement come against our state rival institution. Having been born in 1973, I had yet to experience a loss to Auburn University, and though the Tigers proved to be a most formidable opponent on that day, the 1981 Iron Bowl would not be my first taste of intrastate defeat.

The setting was perfect with the temperature in the 50s, a slight breeze from the southwest, and virtually the entire country hoping and praying that Coach Bryant would make history. I remember Alabama quarterback, Alan Gray, leading the Tide on a beautiful 85-yard drive for a touchdown. I also remember my favorite player, quarterback, #11 Ken Coley, executing a shuffle pass for a score, and everyone recalls Walter Lewis later finding Jesse Bendross deep over the middle to put the game out of reach.

As the final seconds ticked away and it became apparent that Amos Alonzo Staggs' record would fall, I recall Coach Bryant's players lifting him onto their shoulders for a ride to midfield. Though he was a staunch Auburn fan, I will always appreciate my dad putting me on his shoulders so that I could observe this momentous occasion, and will forever be grateful for him enduring my constant desire to talk about this game whenever football was discussed. Put simply, it was # 315, and I was there.

It has been almost 25 years since that fateful Christmas when I received my first Alabama shirt. A quarter-century later, seven years of which I spent as an undergraduate and graduate student at The Capstone, I am more passionate and enthusiastic about The University than ever before. As I carried my son to his first Alabama game last fall, I took pride in knowing that game was the first of many which he and I will attend together as we watch the Tide prove year after year why it has the richest tradition in all of college football.

Though many fans of lesser programs scoff at tradition, there is but one thing that can be said in response. While you may argue about tradition, you cannot argue with it, and those who don't have it probably never will. As such, it comes as no surprise that the diplomas hanging on my office wall bear the name of but one institution, our state's school, THE University of Alabama. Roll Tide!

Jarrod Braxton Bazemore '95 & '98
Birmingham, Alabama

Michael, Michelle and David Proctor

*"I put my head in my hands and refused to watch.
As I would later see on the replay of the game, the
kick sailed through the uprights with plenty of
room to spare."*

*– Michelle Proctor*

———— $\mathcal{A}$ ————

# CONVERSION

I have to be honest and tell you that I actually grew up as an Auburn fan. Please don't think badly of me as we all know how childhood can be confusing and often times you don't figure out who you "really" are until your college years. For me, my conversion began the second Gene Stallings walked into my home when I was a junior in high school. The funny thing was that he was not there to see me, but he had as much of a profound impact on my college decision as he did my brother.

You see, Coach Stallings was at my home to recruit my brother to kick for the University of Alabama. I remember it like it was yesterday. We couldn't tell anyone about his upcoming visit because we didn't want people showing up at our house for autographs. He arrived in the evening and my brother, my parents and I all sat in the living room trying to make Coach Stallings feel as welcomed a guest as possible. My mom had fixed him coffee and served some cheesecake made by a co-worker of my dad's. My brother is a pretty quiet person and striking up a conversation with him can sometimes be difficult, so to break the ice, Coach Stallings started asking me questions. He asked me what my favorite subject in high school was, and I responded with Spanish. He smiled and began to tell me about how he had a ranch in Paris, Texas, and he actually knew some Spanish as well. He proceeded to say words and phrases in Spanish and would pause to see if I could translate them. This went on for about a minute until he uttered (in his low southern drawl) the phrase "venido aqui." I thought for a minute but couldn't recall what the phrase meant in English. I told him I didn't know what it meant. His response was "come here."

I paused for a second and thought maybe the phrase was a little inappropriate so he wanted to whisper it in my ear (remember, this is my first introduction to Coach Stallings). I got out of my chair and walked over to him. He looked up from his cup of tea with some confusion and asked "can I do something for you young lady?" I responded, "You said to come here." He smiled and gave a chuckle and proceeded to explain that the Spanish phrase "venido aqui" means "come here" in English.

I turned beet red and began to walk back to my chair. As I did, I glanced at my brother who was about as red as I was, but it was not from embarrassment. His facial expression said it all…"if you don't sit down in that chair and shut up, I will show you what a football feels like as it's kicked through the uprights!!" Needless to say, I let the rest of my family converse with Coach Stallings that night, but I will never forget how pleasant a man he was and how he took the time to be interested in me…even for a short time. I would be a Bama fan from that day on.

My brother signed a scholarship with Alabama that spring and became the starting kicker his freshman year. I can remember how nervous and excited I was before his first game against Vanderbilt. I was sitting with my parents in the stands, and as the team came onto the field for kickoff, my brother broke the huddle in his new crimson jersey. My mother and I held each other's hand and braced ourselves for the kickoff. The next thing we knew, the kickoff sailed into the end zone and we were hugging each other and crying as if he had just kicked the game winning field goal for the national championship. We were so proud of him for having the chance to put on that crimson jersey, much less actually get on the field and play for the Tide.

That next fall I enrolled at the University of Alabama. Most people would say I did because my brother was playing for the Tide (which is mostly true), but as I mentioned earlier, my conversion really happened with that first visit from Coach Stallings. It was like he embodied everything that was great about Alabama, all rolled into one amazing person. He was a simple man that had one focus…to be the best at everything he did and do it with respect for those who came before him, humility for the opportunity he had been given, passion for the tradition he represented, and a deep caring for everyone involved with moving that tradition forward. That meeting is when I decided to attend Alabama. I can only imagine how the players Coach Stallings recruited felt about him if I was that affected by just one meeting.

I am quite certain any freshman player that attends the University of Alabama to play football is not prepared for the attention they will receive as a player. My indoctrination to the "relative up in the stands" club was quick and somewhat painful my freshman year. I was sitting in the student section with my date (also a freshman), and more specifically, I was sitting in the fraternity section. I remember my brother coming onto the field to attempt about a 40-yard field goal. He missed it, and before I could even think about how disappointed he must have been, I heard from up above me, "Proctor you suck! You couldn't kick water if you were standing in a puddle!" As I turned to give this guy an earful about how he should remember that he is up in the stands pulling for the Tide because he wasn't good enough to be on the field, my date grabbed my arm and pleaded with me not to say anything. Let's just say that senior fraternity members don't take kindly to being put in their place by a pledge's date.

I refrained from telling that guy off, but I noticed that the group behind me had gotten awfully quiet. I could hear some whispering going on behind me, and before I knew it, the senior was tapping me on the shoulder and apologizing for his comments about my brother. I told him not to worry about it, but let's just say that I have a deep appreciation and understanding every time the camera shows Brodie Croyle's father in the stands with his head set on listening to the game (more like drowning out the fans).

I have some wonderful memories from being at Alabama as well as watching my brother kick for the Tide, but my favorite game had to be Bama vs. Georgia in 1994. I remember being excited because it was an ESPN game and therefore the first night game of the season. I met my boyfriend at his apartment late that afternoon, and we proceeded over to the Phi Mu house for the traditional (and now very missed) game day meal: fried chicken with mac and cheese, squash casserole and of course, the ever-favorite Zebra pie. We then made our way over to the RV where my parents usually tailgated and spent some time visiting with relatives and friends. When we entered Bryant Denny, it was electric!

Again, it was the first night game of the season, the weather was perfect, and the Bama Nation had all day to get fired up for the game. All Bama fans remember that game – the fact that Eric Zeier came into the game looking to break the all-time SEC record for passing yards, and the fact that Alabama was known more as a running team than a passing team and that Jay Barker (while a great winner) was known more for his leadership than his passing ability. I was so proud of the Bama players that night because of the way they kept battling back and refusing to give into the "mighty" Georgia offense. At the end of the game, after Jay Barker had thrown for more yards than Eric Zeier and had a career game and after the team had battled back to come within striking distance of the win, it would come down to one kick.

I was sitting in the end zone just to the left of the goal post the kick would eventually sail through, and we were on the first row pressed up against the rail in front of us. I was so nervous when my brother ran out onto the field that I didn't want to watch. One of my friends turned to me just before the kick and explained, "Proctor, if your brother misses this kick you're going over the rail!" He was kidding...I think. I put my head in my hands and refused to watch. As I would later see on the replay of the game, the kick sailed through the uprights with plenty of room to spare. I heard the crowd explode and hoped that my intuition was right. All of a sudden I was being picked up! I thought to myself, "this is it, he missed the kick and I'm going over the rail!" I quickly realized that I was being picked up in celebration because the kick was good and we had won the game.

A sea of plastic cups began to rain down throughout the student section, and I don't think you truly experienced the celebration if you didn't come out of the stadium with some form of "cup" injury. After what seemed like a million Rammer Jammers, I made my way down to the tunnel where I met up with my family, and we waited for my brother to appear. He walked out and was immediately swarmed by a mob of Bama fans begging for his autograph. My parents and I just sat back and smiled (actually I cried) and watched him receive the well-deserved attention he had earned that night.

I am so proud of my brother for what he accomplished playing for The University, but to be honest, it would not have mattered if he hadn't played one snap. You see, it's because of my brother that I met some of my best friends in the world. It's because of my brother I have some of my best memories

I will always cherish, and it's because of my brother that Gene Stallings came to our house that night, rescued me from a decision to go to the plains, and made me into a life long Alabama fan. Thank you, Michael.

Michelle Proctor '97
Birmingham, Alabama

The Proctor Family at '92 SEC Championship
David, Michelle, Jeanette, Michael and Bob

Clint and Anne Lovette in Fenway Park
Boston, Massachusetts

*"I love the fact that Alabama fans impress everyone in the country with their loyalty and participation. And I absolutely love the fact that I can wake up every morning, have my cup of tradition, my helping of SEC and National Championships, and a side of not even acknowledging who Auburn is."*

*- Clint Lovette*

# CURSE OF THE BAMBINO?

I can honestly say that I have never quite "gotten" Auburn fans until I took my first trip to Boston and spent a few days in Cape Cod. I know what you are thinking; Boston and Cape Cod? How can those Yankees possibly compare to Auburn fans? Bear with me. I'll explain.

My wife and I were privileged enough to be invited to a good friend's family home on Cape Cod, and we gladly accepted. We went with another good friend and his wife and decided to spend a couple of days in Boston before we went out to the Cape. Boston is a great town and an even better sports town. It was Labor Day weekend, and all you could hear on the sports talk shows up there was about the Red Sox... not the Patriots... not even a mention... it was all Red Sox. I actually admired these fans for their dedication to their team and felt a little like I was back at home listening to passionate football fans call into the talk radio shows (except that you can't really understand the people up there.)

As I started listening to the callers on the radio, I couldn't believe how down trodden they were and the "Woe is me" attitude they had. Not one person called in and said, "You know, I think we are starting to play some good ball, and I think we may have a shot at the playoffs". It was all about how we should have done this, or do you remember how close we were this year. It suddenly struck me... I was listening to Auburn fans! The similarities were too close for me to ignore.

You see... Red Sox fans are always talking about what might have been. If they had only made this play, or won this game, and especially how MUCH THEY HATE THE YANKEES! They go into every season with the expectation and hope that they will have some great moments, but they never expect to have a really great season, and of course, they never expect to WIN IT ALL. This attitude defines who a Red Sox fan is. If and when they do win the World Series, I reckon that half of the Red Sox fans will disappear because they won't have the camaraderie of tailgating, going to a sports bar, calling into a talk radio show, wallowing (a true southern word) in their own despair, and complaining about the Yankees. Basically, a Red Sox fan wakes up worried and complaining about what the Yankees are doing, while a Yankees fan wakes up and has a cup of tradition, a helping of World Series Championships, and a side of not even acknowledging who the Red Sox are.

Now let me clarify. I am neither a Yankees fan nor a Red Sox fan, but as I drove through Boston listening to the radio, I could not get over the comparisons of the Red Sox fan to the agricultural knock-off down the road fan (in case any Auburn fans are reading... that's you.) The comparison was made even clearer when we actually went to Cape Cod and had to search for a sports bar that would have the Alabama vs. UCLA game. When we got to the bar, the Red Sox fans were in full force, as there was a game in progress, and while I don't remember whom they were playing, I remember thinking how negative their outlook on the game was, and they were winning it! As I listened to the conversations, I was amazed at how many times I heard the Yankees mentioned. Once again, I came back to thinking about Auburn fans and how they love to relish in a bad game or season that the Tide might have and talk about how "if Bama wouldn't have had the Bear, we would have as much tradition as Alabama" (sort of like the Yankees having "all the money" and George Steinbrenner.)

Clint and Anne Lovette with Matt and Noelle Ward touring
Cape Cod, MA on Harleys

Even though we lost that game to UCLA, I left the bar with a sense of relief – relief that I was not an Auburn or Red Sox fan, and I would not spend the rest of my life talking about the "Curse of the Bambino," or especially, "The Curse of the Bear." I love the fact that I was blessed with enough intelligence to become a Bama fan and attend school there. I love the fact that Alabama fans impress everyone in the country with their loyalty and participation. And I absolutely love the fact that I can wake up every morning, have my cup of tradition, my helping of SEC and National Championships, and a side of not even acknowledging who Auburn is.

Clint Lovette '98
Birmingham, Alabama

Photo submitted by Elise Renzetti

1934 Red Sox in Tuscaloosa
Alabama 3 - Red Sox 11
Pictured – Red Sox pitcher Herb Pennock

Jimmy and Kent Gidley at the 1996 Iron Bowl
Alabama 24 – Auburn 23
Legion Field – Birmingham, Alabama
November 23, 1996

*"I never got to see Kent run onto the fresh grass at Bryant Denny Stadium donning a Crimson jersey; however, I can proudly say that I have watched Kent run up and down the field probably more than anyone associated with the Alabama football program within the past 20 years."*

*– Jimmy Gidley*

—— *A* ——

# THAT'S MY BOY

I received my Bachelor's degree from The University in 1964 and my Master's degree the following year. My son, Kent, was born not long after that, and like many other youngsters whose parents bleed crimson and white, it was early in Kent's childhood when it became apparent that he too would love the Tide.

The setting was 1976, just after Kent had turned 10 years old. As my wife, Joan, my daughter, Wendy, and I shopped in the souvenir store, which was then located on the main level of Coleman Coliseum, I allowed Kent to walk out into the lobby where he looked at the numerous trophies contained in the glass cases. When Joan, Wendy, and I finished shopping, we joined Kent in the lobby where we immediately noticed that he was out of breath and virtually unable to speak. Once I was finally able to calm Kent, he informed me that while we were in the store, Coach Bryant had walked into the lobby, shook Kent's hand, and told him to have a good day. To say those few seconds Coach Bryant took to speak to my young son forever changed my son's life is a vast understatement. From that day forward, Kent vowed he would someday play football for the Crimson Tide.

As the years passed, Kent and I attended countless games together as The University added to its hearty supply of SEC and national championships. As Kent progressed in school, it unfortunately became apparent that regardless of Kent's efforts, some subjects were simply more difficult than others, and that Kent suffers from a learning disability. With hard work and extra effort, Kent graduated from high school in 1984. Though a fine athlete in his own right, Kent, like most young boys, would never live out his dream of playing football for the Tide; however, with the exact same spirit Kent dealt with his learning disability, Kent refused to give up on his dream of one day being part of the greatest program in all of college football.

After a short tenure at a junior college, Kent approached me about enrolling at The Capstone. At first, I confess I was reluctant, as The University's academic standards are tough and unforgiving, but at last I gave into my earlier resistance, and in 1986, Kent became an incoming freshman at my alma mater. I never got to see Kent run onto the fresh grass at Bryant Denny Stadium donning a Crimson jersey; however, I can proudly say that I have watched Kent run up and down the field probably more than anyone associated with the Alabama football program within the past 20 years.

During the fall before Kent's freshman year, he attended an Alabama game and was given a media pass, which allowed him access to the field. It was there that Kent, equipped with his camera and his talent, photographed one of the greatest moments in Crimson Tide history, Van Tiffin's winning field goal against Auburn. Armed with a portfolio of impressive pictures, it was early in his freshman year when he was asked to join the very program of which he so longed to be a part, and I am proud to say that Kent has for the past 18 years been the sole photographer for The University of Alabama Athletic Department. During that time, if you have looked at a media guide for any University of Alabama sports program, there is an excellent chance that all of the pictures you have seen were taken by my son, Kent Gidley.

Kent graduated from The University with a degree in photography and is married to the former Ka Ka Jones, a

Ka Ka Jones Gidley

former University of Alabama cheerleader. They have two precious daughters, M'Kay and K'Ten, who I feel confident will one day follow in their mother's footsteps as cheerleaders for our school. Kent and his family are members at Big Sandy Baptist Church, where he serves as Deacon as well as Youth Director. In his spare time, Kent regularly speaks to various groups as he endeavors to help others conquer their own learning disabilities. I always knew that Coach Bryant made a difference in young men's lives. I will always be grateful for that moment in 1976 when Coach Bryant stopped and told that young boy in the coliseum lobby to have a good day. He's had good days ever since.

James Gidley '64 & '65
Hokes Bluff, Alabama

Kent and Jimmy Gidley at the Sugar Bowl
Alabama 24 – Arkansas 9
New Orleans, Louisiana
January 1, 1980

Jimmy and Joan Gidley at the 1994 Iron Bowl
Alabama 21 – Auburn 14
Legion Field – Birmingham, Alabama
November 19, 1994

Jennifer Allen Harper

*"Many people hope to get their 15 minutes
of fame but what a claim to fame, huh?
Fortunately, I had no serious injuries – just a bit
of a pulled muscle in my neck and a bruised ego.
I still flinch every time I see one of the players
punt a ball on the sidelines."*

*– Jennifer Allen Harper*

# INCOMING!

I t was the Alabama vs. Auburn game at Legion Field on November 23, 1996, the biggest game of the year for many fans. I was in my third year as a member of the Million Dollar Band Colorguard. The band had just finished pre-game, and we were exiting the field (I just happened to be on the back sideline right in front of the student section). It would be a game special in many ways, including my "15 minutes of fame."

Meanwhile, Hayden Stockton had begun to practice punting on the same sideline. As I was walking off the field, I looked up and noticed one of the Bama cheerleaders giving me this horrified look... and that's when it hit me. One of those practice punts came down and hit me in the back of the head! You have to imagine how it felt... like a ton of bricks hitting me from behind. I stood there for maybe 5 seconds and then just fell over on the field.

All of a sudden, there were tons of people standing over me, "Are you okay? Can you talk? Are you breathing?" It was a bit overwhelming, so I said, "If you would all just step back and let me sit up, I think I'll be okay." I sat up and just sort of put my head in my hands for a second trying to shake it off. Then I noticed this shiny, clean pair of shoes come walking up in front of me. I looked up, and there was Gene Stallings. He looked down at me, smiled and said, "You all right, little lady?" I just stared for a moment and then finally stammered out a "yes." He reached down, helped me up off the ground and gave me a hug. I heard the crowd start to cheer.

It was then I realized the game was delayed while this was going on. The players had already lined up for kick-off, the fans were chanting "Rooooollllll" waiting for the kick, but Gene Stallings walked down to the end of the field to check on me. What a true gentleman. Alabama went on to win the game 24-23, with Freddie Kitchens' 6-yard touchdown pass to Dennis Riddle with 32 seconds to play. Little did I know how important that day would become when Coach Stallings announced his retirement.

After the game, I learned that the television cameras had caught the entire incident, primarily because I began to receive phone calls from people I hadn't seen in years who had seen me on TV.

Many people hope to get their 15 minutes of fame but what a claim to fame, huh? Fortunately, I had no serious injuries – just a bit of a pulled muscle in my neck and a bruised ego. I still flinch every time I see one of the players punt a ball on the sidelines.

Jennifer Allen Harper '98
Birmingham, Alabama

Chris and Jennifer Harper

Mike Kennedy, #26, Alabama Fullback 1978-79

*"Another thing I noticed my first year at Alabama was with how many former players Coach Bryant kept in touch. We would have a team meeting before every practice and it seemed like every meeting he would have a different story about a former player he had just spoken with and how they have gone on to be successful in life."*

*- Mike Kennedy, Alabama Fullback 1978-79*

# TWISTS OF FATE

I can remember as a young child dreaming of playing for the Crimson Tide and Coach Bryant. My first opportunity to meet Coach was when I was in the seventh grade, and my uncle took me to see him. I was a pretty big seventh grader (not much smaller than when I played college ball), and I remember the first thing Coach Bryant said to me was, "Son, you're as big as a skinned mule."

When I entered high school, my dream of playing for Coach Bryant only grew stronger, but my older brother had turned out to be a pretty good athlete as well, so I also dreamed of being on the sidelines with him in college. As fate would have it, my brother went to Florida State to play for Coach Bobby Bowden, and I was left with a decision to make. Both schools were recruiting me, and as much as I loved the Tide, I could not pass up an opportunity to play alongside my brother, so I chose to follow him to FSU.

My first year at Florida State did not go as planned, and I decided to make the tough decision of leaving my brother and transferring to and playing for my first love, the Crimson Tide. I remember showing up for August workouts, and as it is today, you must have a coach's permission to transfer schools and then sit out a year. Coach Bowden had yet to sign my transfer, and I had to miss two-a-days, but all it took was one phone call from Coach Bryant, and we promptly received the necessary paperwork from Coach Bowden.

My first year with Coach Bryant was a true learning experience. I was struck by how many things Coach could be and how he could adapt to different situations. He was tough but fair, a tremendous motivator, a philosopher, and he knew how to press the different buttons on all his players. We would always meet as a team on Wednesday nights, and I remember before the Tennessee game in 1978, he came in and talked to the team about how important winning this game was, the history of the game, as well as what it meant to all of our parents and the fans. At one point during his talk, he got so emotional that he actually started to cry. The team would have taken on an entire army after that meeting, and looking back, I think that was the best example of how Coach could adapt to any situation that presented itself.

Another thing I noticed my first year at Alabama was with how many former players Coach Bryant kept in touch. We would have a team meeting before every practice, and it seemed like every meeting he would have a different story about a former player he had just spoken with and how they have gone on to be successful in life. You could tell how proud of his former players he was, and it truly made you feel like he had your best interest at heart.

Something I think of a lot as a fan of the Tide is when the fourth quarter comes and everyone on the sideline and in the stands raises their four fingers. Many teams have copied this over the years, and I'm not sure how many Bama fans actually realize that the fourth quarter mentality comes from Coach Bryant's years. He would always talk about how important it was to "OWN the fourth quarter," and how "if you are tired during the fourth quarter, your opponent was going to be more tired." During every practice, when the horn would blow signaling the start of the final period of practice, Coach would get on his megaphone and yell "fourth quarter...it's time to get better…we got to get better," and everyone would pick up the intensity of practice no matter how tired and worn out they were. He always talked about expecting the unexpected and that if you worked hard and were prepared, you would never be defeated…on the field or in life.

My first year at Alabama was bittersweet. You see it was 1978, and we had won the National Championship, but since I was only able to practice with the team and not play, I was not eligible to receive a ring. You had to have played for one play during the year.

As a result, I went into spring practice determined to make an impression on the coaches and contribute on the field that next season. That spring, I remember we had a receiver transfer in from California. He was a great athlete and made an immediate impression on the coaching staff. I'm not sure if it was his "left coast" mentality, but he decided he didn't need to practice as much as the rest of us. Coach Bryant would always make out the depth chart for the scrimmages and call them out right before the scrimmage started. He called out this receiver's name and everyone huddled. Coach gave the play to run, and the offense broke the huddle with 10 players and missing a receiver. Coach Bryant blew his whistle and asked where was this certain receiver. The assistant coaches brought to his attention that this player had missed several practices. Coach Bryant called over the manager, told him to go this player's dorm room, pack up his "stuff" and pile it in front of the athletic dorm. "He is no longer on the team." Needless to say, not many players thought about missing practices on Coach Bryant's team.

At the beginning of the 1979 season, the team was excited about the prospect of another great season, and I was excited about the prospect of actually playing. It was the third game of the season, and when I got to my locker, the manager had put a tear away jersey in my locker instead of a regular one. I asked the manager if he had made a mistake, and he said, "No, Coach Bryant told me to give you one."

I was more nervous than I had ever been before a game. As fate would have it, we did not play well, and almost no one played except for the starters. When we scored the last touchdown that game, my roommate, who was the second string fullback, grabbed me and tried to get me to take his place in the extra point. I was about five yards out on the field when I turned to my roommate and told him that there was no way I was going out there because Coach Bryant would have killed me or kicked me off the team, or both. Once again, as fate would have it, we went into practice the Monday after that game, and I blew out my knee in the scrimmage. My season was over having not played a down and our team was going on to win the National Championship. I was not able to participate in a game, thus I did not receive a ring that season either.

Even though we were in the middle of the season, Coach Bryant would come to the hospital in the mornings and sit and talk with me and my parents. It was like you were talking to your next door neighbor and not some legendary figure that would go on to win his sixth National Championship that year. I worked out hard rehabbing my knee throughout the spring and stayed through the summer so I could get ready for the upcoming season. I later learned that the doctors and coaches had known that I would never play football again, but Coach Bryant wanted me to rehab my knee as if I was going to play so that I would not have any long lasting effects from my injury.

While twists of fate may have kept me from reaching my childhood dream of playing in a game for Coach Bryant, I will never forget the lessons I learned from him, being a part of those two great teams, and how much bigger a fan of the Crimson Tide it has made me.

Mike Kennedy
Red Bay, Alabama
Alabama Fullback 1978-79
Lifelong Fan

Len Lee with Coach Paul Bryant
October 29, 1969

*"Suddenly, my dad took my arm and said, 'Come with me, I want you to meet someone.' We walked toward one of the small sales offices and my dad opened the door. I walked in to see a giant man looking at me who said, 'Congratulations on your car son.' There, standing larger than life, was my hero, the one and only – Coach Paul 'Bear' Bryant – and he was handing me a set of keys."*

*- Len Lee*

—— 𝒜 ——

# BEAR'S BUG

On October 29, 1969, I was a 15-year-old high school freshman at Birmingham's Banks High School. My sister was a student at the University of Alabama, so when my parents stated they were going to let me miss school to go visit her the next day, I was excited. Little did I know what was in store for me on that memorable trip to Tuscaloosa. Not only would I receive my first car, but a legend would hand me the keys.

The next day began just like any other except that I was riding to Tuscaloosa instead of school. We arrived in Tuscaloosa around 9 a.m. and went to my sister's place. After eating breakfast, my dad said, "I hear that today is the grand opening of Paul Bryant Volkswagen. You want to go see what they have?"

What 15-year-old wasn't interested in cars, especially when the lot is owned by Bear Bryant? So I said, "Sure".

We arrived at Bear Bryant Volkswagen on McFarland Boulevard and entered the showroom. I walked around looking at the Bugs, Buses and Karmann Ghias. Suddenly, my dad took my arm and said, "Come with me, I want you to meet someone." We walked toward one of the small sales offices and my dad opened the door. I walked in to see a giant man looking at me who said, "Congratulations on your car son." There, standing larger than life, was my hero, the one and only – Coach Paul "Bear" Bryant – and he was handing me a set of keys.

Turned out my dad had set the whole thing up and agreed to purchase the car only if Coach Bryant would be there to greet me with the keys. I remember Coach Bryant being gracious and telling me he had selected one of the new yellow Volkswagens just for me. He wrote on the bill of sale, "Selected by Paul Bryant – Beautiful Yellow - Paul Bryant." He even went out to the car with me while my dad was taking pictures.

I recently found one of those pictures, and I was able to prove what I had been telling people for years. Amazingly, I remembered exactly what I was wearing that day. I've kept that bill of sale receipt over the years, and I'm having it framed with a reprint of the picture I found. The total experience didn't last more than 15 minutes and was over 30 years ago, but I still remember it like it was yesterday.

Len Lee
Birmingham, Alabama

Len Lee's Bill of Sale from Paul Bryant Volkswagen

Chris Hampton at graduation with his mom and dad, Myra and J.W.

*"I never saw Dad as proud as when I walked across the stage at graduation in 1996. His son had graduated from the school he so loved – a first generation Alabama graduate."*

*– Chris Hampton*

---·*A*·---

# FIRST GENERATION GRADUATE

I was the last of four children, and the only boy of parents who simply bled crimson and white. By the time I turned one, I had learned to say, "Ma Ma, Da Da, and Roll Tide," but not necessarily in that order. Mom and Dad had not graduated from The University, but were huge fans and supporters of the school, and they always wanted me to do three things in life -- go to church, give my very best in all I do, and one day attend college at The Capstone.

My childhood was like many others growing up in our state. During the week, there were school and various hobbies, and on the weekends in the fall, we made pilgrimages to legendary Legion Field and Bryant Denny Stadium. It seems like only yesterday. Dad, who was a banker, would take off work early on gameday mornings, fill the car up with gas, and pick me up at home. We would then stop by Jarrod Bazemore's house, my future college roommate and co-author of this book, whom Dad and I rescued from a life filled with orange and blue, and then we'd all head south for the game. En route, we always stopped at Pruetts' Restaurant in Gadsden to get barbeque sandwiches, and rest assured, our trips to the stadium were filled with great food and nonstop talk about Alabama football.

As the years passed and I entered high school, this tradition never changed. Upon graduation and consideration of golfing scholarships at various small colleges, I decided to forego my sporting career and enroll at The University of Alabama. Dad could not have been prouder. In August 1991, Jarrod and I became freshmen at the Capstone – typical freshmen, to say the least. We studied a little and partied a lot. Mom once told someone that those boys only act right when they're asleep, but she wasn't even sure about that, and though I did not live at home anymore, the Hampton Saturday tradition never changed. One could set his clock by it. On gameday mornings, I usually awoke to a knock on the door, where I would find Mom and Dad standing there with huge smiles on their faces and Dad with a bag of barbeque sandwiches in his hand. Though we no longer had the long drive to the stadium to discuss football, we now hashed out that day's game at my kitchen table.

I met my future wife, Shannon Wilder, while a student at The University, and I never saw Dad as proud as when I walked across the stage at graduation in 1996. His son had graduated from the school he so loved – a first generation Alabama graduate. Unfortunately, Dad passed away unexpectedly one month after my graduation, and for a long time after that, I totally lost interest in attending games in the fall. I still loved the Tide, but going to the games did not mean as much as it once did – that was until June 11, 2002, when my son, Chandler, was born. It was then that I quickly discovered that I had the same dreams for Chandler that Dad had for me – go to church, give his best, and graduate from our state school.

Like most Alabama dads, I long for the day when Shannon and I will sit in the stadium and proudly watch Chandler run out of the tunnel wearing a bright crimson jersey ready to propel the Tide onto yet another national championship. However, if that day never comes, I still hope that Chandler will choose to attend my alma mater, and I can only pray that when Shannon and I arrive in Tuscaloosa early on Saturday mornings in the fall, Chandler will be just as happy to see me standing on his doorstep with a smile on my face and a bag of sandwiches in my hand as I was when my dad would visit.

Christopher Wade Hampton '96
Albertville, Alabama

Chandler Hampton, future
All-American and Second Generation Graduate

David Olivet

*"For the first nine years of my life, 'larger than life'*
*was the corn-shaped water tank near the Libby's*
*plant in Rochester, Minnesota or the huge*
*snowfalls that we saw every winter, but after*
*moving to Tuscaloosa and being immersed in*
*the culture of Alabama Football, the phrase*
*took on a whole new meaning."*

*– David Olivet*

# LARGER THAN LIFE

I was raised to be an Alabama fan. One of the oldest photographs of me shows me as a baby lying beside a University of Alabama football with a big smile on my face. No big deal, right? I'm sure there are thousands of pictures of kids with University of Alabama footballs. But, how many of those pictures do you think were taken in the state of Minnesota? That's right – I was born and raised in the Land of 10,000 Lakes – the home of the Jolly Green Giant and the Minnesota Vikings.

Yet through all the winters of six-foot snows and the summers of six-foot mosquitoes, my parents remained true to their southern roots and raised us to be Alabama fans. My brother and I both had Johnny Musso pajamas, complete with the number 22 sewn on the front, and watched every game the Tide played on national TV (which back in the 1970s was usually one per year – a New Year's Day bowl game). Of course, my little Minnesota friends didn't appreciate the mystique of college football. I wouldn't either if my choices were Mankato State or the Minnesota Golden Gophers. Nothing against either school, but when it comes to the gridiron, they don't quite have the same tradition as the University of Alabama. My buddies were either into ice hockey or the Minnesota Vikings. Bud Grant, Fran Tarkenton and Alan Page were the gods of the schoolyard, but Bear Bryant, Joe Namath and Lee Roy Jordan reigned supreme in our house.

Knowing the tradition, names and all the lyrics to "Yea, Alabama" is simply "head knowledge." You can learn it, but you can't really understand it if you've never experienced it. It wasn't until my family moved to Tuscaloosa in 1979 when I was 10 years old that I was able to truly understand in my heart what Alabama football is all about.

Dad took me to see Bama play Virginia Tech that year – my first game ever. We got to the stadium about two hours before kickoff so that we could watch the team warm up and see the Million Dollar Band march in. Dad played tenor saxophone in the Million Dollar Band in 1964, and if I had a nickel for every time I've heard him tell how they spelled out the score, time and temperature during the halftime show, I'd be a wealthy man. But hearing him tell about it is not the same as hearing that band filling up Bryant-Denny Stadium with the familiar strains of "Yea, Alabama." As the crowd inside got larger, the band got louder and the energy in the stadium intensified. I had never seen so many people, heard so much noise, or felt so much excitement. When the team finally burst out of the tunnel, I started cheering with everything I had and didn't stop until the Tide had beaten the Hokies 31-7. My indoctrination was complete. I had been baptized into Alabama football – washed in the Crimson Tide.

When I was in elementary school, Tuscaloosa City Schools used student teachers from The University on a regular basis and Verner Elementary was no exception. One year, we were fortunate enough to have an Alabama football player as a student P.E. teacher. His name was Steve Rhoden, a backup quarterback for the Tide, and as I later found, a member of our church. Steve always went out of his way to speak to me at church, and as the year went on, we developed a great friendship. One spring afternoon, he invited my younger brother Jeff and me to come to see the Tide practice. It was tough for a couple of kids to understand what was going on, but we knew one thing – the guy in the tower was Bear Bryant, the greatest coach in college football, overseeing his world like Zeus on Olympus. There was no doubt in our minds whose world this was. After practice, Steve brought us into the locker room to meet some of the players. Never in my life had I met men of this stature. Their hands swallowed mine with every handshake, and I felt tiny in their presence. While Steve showered, Jeff and I waited outside the locker room. That's when it happened. We were standing in a long hallway when the double doors at the other end opened revealing the silhouette of a man in a baseball cap – obviously not a player. As he moved closer to us, we realized that this was the heart of Alabama football. It was Bear Bryant. We both stood with our jaws on the floor until he slowly walked up to us, bent down and shook our hands. He asked us our names and if we enjoyed practice and then gave us his autograph. Then he continued down the hall. It was a brief encounter, but anytime I hear the phrase "a brush with greatness," I always think about the day I met "The Bear."

For the first nine years of my life, "larger than life" was the corn-shaped water tank near the Libby's plant in Rochester, Minnesota or the huge snowfalls that we saw every winter, but after moving to Tuscaloosa and being immersed in the culture of Alabama Football, the phrase took on a whole new meaning.

David Olivet '92
Birmingham, Alabama

Scott Mize and Major Tim Kimbrough

*"It was then I realized that things were going to be all right. Life would go on, and the pastime of sports would, as well. It was okay to laugh and have fun again. It's odd how the smallest things in life can help us see the whole picture. That day in September 2001 changed everything, but it didn't change who we are. And we certainly should never stop cheering Roll Tide Roll!"*

*– Scott Mize*

# SMELLS LIKE
# TEAM SPIRIT

I have so many memories of Alabama football, so it's hard to think of just one that sticks out more than the rest. The strongest recent memory was the first game I attended after the terrorist attacks of September 11, 2001. I was living in Atlanta at the time, so it was the following season before I made it to a game. Alabama was playing Mississippi State in an afternoon game at Bryant-Denny Stadium. My cousin, a major in the United States Air Force, was in town, so we thought it was a good chance to see a game together. A graduate of Michigan State, he understands what good football is all about. It was a great day for a game.

After September 11th, the debate was ongoing about whether or not sports should continue as if nothing had happened. We had all asked ourselves if it was okay to laugh, to have fun, to get on with life as we knew it before. Some suggested sports should not take on as much meaning as they previously had. With this being my first game since 9/11, I found myself asking these questions. I was unsure how it would feel, or how I would react to be at a game again.

On the drive down, my mother called my cell phone several times to make sure we didn't forget anything. She reminded me where to park and to call my sister when I got there. My sister was a student at that time, and we would usually park at her friend's apartment near The Corner Store.

The last time my mom called, she only said one thing: "If you park where we normally do, don't step in dog crap." I hung up in disbelief. She had called me to remind me of this? As I hung up, I turned to my cousin, "You will not believe what she just called for." Since our mothers are sisters, he understood completely, and we both could not stop laughing. I didn't give her advice a second thought. I turned up the radio and continued down I-20/59 toward the Capstone.

We pulled into Tuscaloosa and got to our parking place about an hour before kickoff. After stepping out of the car, I stretched my legs and proceeded with the normal checklist. Wallet? Tickets? Sunglasses? Cell phone? Keys? Tickets? (Very Important!). I had used the remote button to open the trunk so Tim could take inventory of the food and drinks we had brought with us. After a few moments, Tim asked, "What is that smell?!"

I hadn't noticed anything and was trying to think of what in my trunk could be the source. His head popped up over the trunk, and we looked at each other. He quickly checked his shoes and shook his head as he looked back at me. I looked down at my feet and didn't see anything. Then I moved my foot. There it was. When I looked back at Tim, he could see the horror in my eyes and began to laugh as hard as I have ever heard him laugh. I, of course, was not amused.

We have all heard that we should "listen to our mothers" and that "mother knows best." Even the Bear came back to Alabama because "Mamma called." This, however, was too much. I had on shoes with thin, deep-treaded soles, so there was no way I was going to get all of it out. We continued to laugh about it as we made our way to the stadium.

Major Tim Kimbrough

As we stood waiting for the team to run on the field, my mind wandered back to the events of September 11th. We noticed two armed men standing atop the roof overhang above the new upper deck. It was definitely a different feeling. Watching the Million Dollar Band sound the call for our team to make its way on the field, I could only think of one thing.

Can the girl behind me smell the stuff on my shoe as much as I can?

It was then I realized that things were going to be all right. Life would go on, and the pastime of sports would as well. It was okay to laugh and have fun again. It's odd how the smallest things in life can help us see the whole picture. That day in September 2001 changed everything, but it didn't change who we are. And we certainly should never stop cheering Roll Tide Roll!

W. Scott Mize '98
Birmingham, Alabama

Photo submitted by Elise Renzetti

Denny Chimes

Front: Louis Palestini (grandfather), Wayne Palestini (uncle) and Joseph Tombrello (dad) Back: Mike Palestini (cousin) and Joe Tombrello

*"Today is my wedding day. …As we enter our reception… we will do it to the University of Alabama fight song, and I know that my grandfather and my family will all be smiling… because we all love The University."*

*– Dr. Joseph Tombrello*

——— 𝒜 ———

# FAMILY TRADITION

In the fall of 1931, a man from Hoboken, New Jersey, enrolled at the University of Alabama. That man was my grandfather, Louis Palestini. Four years later, in 1935, my grandfather left UA with a degree in engineering, but more importantly, he left with a sense of pride, accomplishment and a love for the school that would continue to spread throughout our family. For those who attended The Capstone and even those who did not, my family would carry on the tradition for years to come.

His son, Wayne Palestini, continued in his father's footsteps and likewise attended the University of Alabama. I was a young boy then, but I could see the pride in my grandfather's eyes when his son graduated from the University of Alabama and went on to dental school at UAB.

I also went on to enroll at The University in the fall of 1993, and I can remember my uncle (now a dentist in Birmingham) telling me about a conversation he had with my grandfather a few months before he passed away. They sat and talked about fishing, life and what the University of Alabama still meant to them. My grandfather spoke about how he was so happy that he had the opportunity to see his son and his grandson attend The University and how he expected nothing less from his grandson than to graduate from UA and go on to become a doctor.

Later that year, my grandfather passed away. While at the funeral, my cousin Mike Palestini pulled me aside to give me something my grandfather had given him. My grandfather had given his oldest grandson his 1935 University of Alabama class ring. The ring was worn. The one-time engraving of Denny Chimes and the date – 1935 – were barely visible. Only the L and P of Louis Palestini could still be read on the inside of the ring. My grandfather wore this ring with great pride and had saved it for his oldest grandson to have. Mike then did something that blew me away. Standing in Elmwood Cemetery, burying my grandfather, Mike gave me my grandfather's 1935 class ring. Mike did not attend Alabama but chose to run his own business instead. Mike told me that he felt I deserved to have the ring and that my grandfather would smile knowing that he had given it to me. I cried that day, tears that I have never cried before and tears that I cry now as I write this.

Today is my wedding day. This evening I will be surrounded by people I love. My parents, sisters, aunts, uncles, cousins, and friends will be around me, and when I look out into the audience, I'll see my cousin Mike, and over his shoulder somewhere I will see my grandfather. As we enter our reception as Dr. Joseph Anthony Tombrello and Dr. Carrie Francis Tombrello, we will do it to the University of Alabama fight song, and I know that my grandfather and my family will all be smiling… because we all love The University.

Dr. Joseph Tombrello '97
Birmingham, Alabama

Joe's Groom Cake

# SOME THINGS
# NEVER CHANGE

As a young boy growing up in the late 1970s, I kept a strict ritual on Saturdays in the fall. Like the team, I awoke around 9 a.m. I would eat a late breakfast while focusing on my game responsibilities, and I would then adorn my game day attire and await kickoff. It is a time I still fondly remember.

My uniform consisted of a pair of faded blue jeans, a half sleeve crimson t-shirt and occasional piece of tape around my wrist, or sweat bands if I could find them. There was nothing fancy about it, but it gave me the power and strength that I needed each week to save victory from the jaws of defeat and propel the Tide onto yet another national championship.

I would begin every game sitting in front of the TV, just hoping to see my hero, #42 Major Ogilvie, break away for a touchdown. Even though I was just a child, I would soon become too nervous to watch the game and would grab my football and take to the front yard so that I could get into the action. There, I would pretend I was Major Ogilvie where I would score touchdown after touchdown until I would either collapse from exhaustion or my mom would call me in for dinner. Not surprisingly, Major was never brought down in my front yard, and the Tide never lost – basically the same result from the actual games I was too nervous to watch.

As I become older, I often reflect on my youth, especially the memories of me pretending I was Major Ogilvie on those hot Saturday afternoons in the fall. Many may wonder and even deem it strange for a 9 year old boy to be nervous while watching a football game, because after all, isn't it just a game? Those of such a mind-set obviously did not grow up in Alabama and are certainly not fans of the greatest program in all of college football. Put simply, Alabama football has not, is not, and never will be just a game. It's much, much more. It's a way of life. You are born with it, you die with it, and your happiness during those moments in between greatly depends on it.

Over a quarter of a century later, I am much too old to take to the front yard and pretend I'm Major Ogilvie, though I must confess the urge hits me occasionally. Although everyone changes with time, I am proud to say that I still wake up nervous on Saturday mornings in the fall, and I hope and pray that part of me never changes.

Kevin Turner '95
Centre, Alabama

Anna Marie Ayers and William Ross Ayers

*"Although I laughed, I thought that my noble efforts to instruct William on the merits of Tennessee were about to be rewarded. I asked William which team he wanted to be. He announced, "I'm Bwody Coral and I'm da good guy! You are Cassey Closen, and you're da bad guy." With that, he sprinted across the room in a 'Row Tie' war chant and delivered a ferocious shoulder tackle to my leg."*

*– Daniel Ayers*

# A TALE OF TWO UNCLES

I concede that I am not an Alabama fan, but I feel compelled to tell this story on behalf of my three year old Crimson and White nephew William Ayers, whose verbal skills are still a work in progress.

My brother and sister-in-law celebrated the birth of two beautiful babies October 23, 2000. William Ross Ayers, weighed in at 6 pounds 2 ounces and Anna Marie Ayers at 5 pounds 13 ounces. It is a wonderful feeling to become an uncle to one baby, but becoming an uncle to twins is all the more special. I shared this first-time uncle experience with my sister-in-law's brother Scott. This shared pride in these wonderful kids would soon develop into a friendly rivalry.

While it's great to become an uncle, a competitive urge somehow takes over to become the favorite uncle. In becoming the favorite uncle, you want the children to appreciate the things that you hold dear. You want them to appreciate and learn your values, favorite activities, and of course collegiate allegiance. Scott is a very laidback and patient fellow, but a staunch Alabama fan. I, on the other hand, tend to be more of a talker, outlandish at times, and grew up with a fondness for that school a few miles to the northeast in Knoxville. This is really where the Uncle Scott vs. Uncle Illia (or "Uncle Cot" vs. "Uncle Ittle" as the twins affectionately refer to us) rivalry began.

I held an early favorite uncle lead over Scott as he lived a few hours away in Atlanta. I approached Christmas and birthdays as an opportunity to score major points with William and Anna. Their Christmas at age two was an especially crucial gift year as it was the first time the twins seemed to perceive the wonder of a gift and from whom it was given. I was sure that the matching tricycles would be a major hit. I took great joy in watching these little dudes enjoy the gifts as they sped across the floor. I felt very comfortable with my choice until my brother explained that Scott would be arriving late that evening due to his job. When I asked where Scott was working, my brother explained that he had taken a management position with Wal-Mart. I was overcome with a sinking feeling. I felt the same sensation that Jerry Seinfeld expressed each time he exclaimed the word, "Newman!" I pictured Scott smiling ear to ear as he purchased buggy loads of gifts with a huge employee discount.

Scott arrived with gifts in hand. As the kids opened their gifts, I felt relief because the tricycles were yet to be trumped. But as William opened the final present from Uncle Scott, to my dismay, I witnessed Scott's launch of a new offensive front in the war of uncles. William proudly toured the living room sporting his new Crimson Tide sweatshirt. I was then flanked by my step-father and sister-in-law teaching this impressionable child to say Roll Tide. The incessant chatter of "Row Tie" filled the living room for the remainder of the evening as young William sped around the floor on his tricycle.

In the summer of 2003, Scott moved to Birmingham to seek new employment. He moved in with my brother and sister-in-law to prepare for his job search in town. I could only imagine the Crimson propaganda that would follow. I was also experiencing a new beginning in the start-up of a business that would eliminate much of the free time that I previously enjoyed. Despite the lack of time, I tried to make the best of my brief interactions with William and Anna. I tried to convince them that Orange was really their favorite color and that Smokey was actually much nicer and tougher than Big Al. I tried to instill in them the value of quarterback Casey Clausen. Scott, on the other hand, spent most Saturdays watching Alabama football with William.

The months passed along to Christmas 2003. Once again, we spoiled the twins with the best gifts that we could find and afford. The entire family (Scott included) was relaxed in the living room as William and I played with his brand new four-wheel drive army jeep. William suddenly jumped up and proclaimed, "Wets Pway Footbawl!" By this time, he had developed a bit of a southern drawl in his three year old voice which brought laughter to the room. Although I laughed, I thought that my noble efforts to instruct William on the merits of Tennessee were about to be rewarded. I asked William which team he wanted to be. He announced, "I'm Bwody Coral and I'm da good guy! You are Cassey Closen, and you're da bad guy." With that, he sprinted across the room in a "Row Tie" war chant and delivered a ferocious shoulder tackle to my leg. At first, the humor of this three year old's proclamation and subsequent tackle was too funny to resist side splitting laughter. But the realization had set in that I had been outmatched by the other uncle. To add to my shame, shouts of Roll Tide rang out from several of my Tide supporting family members. Meanwhile, Scott sat silently with a glowing smirk. "Newman!"

I later found out that Scott had an accomplice. This accomplice was a four year old named Luke. Luke worked covertly to influence William's allegiance to Alabama while they attended church day school.

Indeed, I lost that battle. However, opportunity still exists. Anna is still undecided in her collegiate loyalties. Anna is very much a girly girl and has lately expressed great interest in becoming a "Chea Leaduh." I bet you can guess what she'll be getting for her birthday.

I. Daniel Ayers
Birmingham, Alabama

William Ross Ayers

Brian and Keisha Limbaugh with Brooke and Chad Hopper
Tailgating before Iron Bowl 2002

*"We stayed in the stadium and cheered for another hour or so as the Tiger faithful fortified around their beloved Toomer's Corner. Everyone soon began to chant, "SEC, SEC" as we all knew we just won the West and earned a spot in the SEC Championship game. Yes, indeed, we were headed to Atlanta."*

*– Brian Limbaugh*

—— $\mathcal{A}$ ——

# VICTORY
# ON THE PLAINS

The year was 1999, and the college football season was coming to an end. The Crimson Tide was looking for its first win at its arch rival's home field and a chance to win a spot in the SEC Championship game. Coach Mike DuBose was recapturing the pride and swagger of old, while saving his job at the same time.

This was my third Iron Bowl game to see in person; however, it was the first time to see the game played in Auburn. The first two were successful comeback wins for Bama at Legion Field, and the third followed suit. My undergraduate roommate, Chad Hopper, was attending law school at Alabama and was nice enough to provide me with a ticket for the big game. This was my eighth game of the year to see in person, preceded by the huge win down in the Swamp against the Florida Gators.

I drove down to The Plains the night before the game to stay with another friend of mine who, of course, was an Auburn fan, before meeting Chad on game day. The night was full of anticipation and excitement. At last, the sun came up, and it was time to don the crimson and white gear and prepare for war. My friend and I left his apartment and went our separate ways, and I eagerly proceeded to find my Bama friend somewhere on the campus of the enemy. Of course, I was taunted quite a bit by many obnoxious Tiger fans as I made my way toward the stadium; however, I held my head high with my crimson and white shaker in my hand, beaming all the confidence and pride in the world for my Tide.

I found Chad, and we entered the stadium together. What an atmosphere! There is nothing like the Iron Bowl. Those biased commentators can say Ohio State and Michigan, Army and Navy, or Notre Dame and their grand Irish opponent are the best rivalries in football, but Brian Limbaugh and many, many more beg to differ. There is no other rivalry in sports that compares to Alabama and Auburn. It's "tradition" versus "we wished we had a tradition." It's a war.

Back to the game. We took our seats in the Bama section, cheering on our Tide players as they were warming up, literally feeling The Million Dollar Band as they played our fight song, "Yea Alabama." My heart was pounding, the butterflies were fluttering, and it was time to get it on.

The game was a battle from beginning to end. Auburn took the lead into halftime, but I had complete confidence that our guys would come back. Ok, I was a little nervous and worried. I mean we had not won a game on The Plains yet. The key word was "yet." The Tide came out in the second half as a team possessed. Kindal Moorehead had a key sack for a safety and Shaun Alexander, the True Heisman in all of our hearts, took over and ran the ball down the throat of the Auburn defense. When the final buzzer sounded, it was the University of Alabama on top, 28-17, and the chant of "Hey Auburn, Hey Auburn, Hey Auburn, We just beat the hell out of you, Ramma Jamma Yellow Hamma, Give 'em hell Alabama" rang through the crowd. The Bama section was going crazy as we had just witnessed the Tide's first victory on The Plains. We stayed in the stadium and cheered for another hour or so as the Tiger faithful fortified around their beloved Toomer's Corner.

Everyone soon began to chant, "SEC, SEC" as we all knew we just won the West and earned a spot in the SEC Championship game. Yes, indeed, we were headed to Atlanta.

To say the least, this game goes down as one of my all-time favorites. There is nothing like a win over Auburn, and it's even sweeter to be a part of the Bama family watching it in person. The victory on the Plains was an event I will never forget.

Roll Tide!

Brian Limbaugh
Birmingham, Alabama

Like Father, Like Son
Andy Martin at the Georgia Dome after throwing passes
to son, Matthew, while trying to get Brett Favre's attention

*"As the weeks passed following my performance of
a lifetime, I awaited the call from my dad's friend
to tell me how the Bear was searching for that
tremendous mystery receiver he saw catching
passes in the front yard."*

*— Andy Martin*

# HEY BEAR...
# LOOK AT ME!

I attended my first University of Alabama football game during the spectacular season of 1971. My father took great pride in taking our entire family to the homecoming game against the University of Miami Hurricanes. It was expected to be a big win since Alabama was undefeated. As expected, the Crimson Tide destroyed the hapless Hurricanes to seemingly cap off the perfect day, but what made the trip so special was the whole homecoming and Crimson Tide experience. I remember fondly as my father took me into a sporting goods store and got me a number 22 jersey in honor of my favorite player, the Italian Stallion Johnny Musso. In addition to that, we went to the Sigma Nu House and had a buffet lunch and got to hear my father catch up on his war stories with all his friends. On my way through the parking lot to the game, I found a $10 bill which was an enormous sum of money in 1971 to a 9-year-old boy. It was truly a day of enchantment.

However, after the game I realized that I was in for an even bigger treat. We went to spend the night with a long-time family friend of my parents who lived in an upscale neighborhood in Tuscaloosa. After we got there, I noticed a nice home to the left with a pool in back and inquired as to who the neighbor was. They mentioned to me that the next-door neighbor was none other than Bear Bryant himself. I was so excited I couldn't stand it. I immediately asked if we could go knock on Bear's door so that I could introduce myself to him. Being from Dothan, we were so neighborly I just couldn't imagine why he wouldn't want to meet the friends of his next-door neighbor. Everyone assured me that Bear was probably tired after the game, and we should not knock on his door.

The next morning I woke up excitedly thinking that now was the time to go meet the Bear himself. Again, I was discouraged from knocking on his door, so finally in desperation, I thought of the only way that I knew to get the Bear's attention. I was playing wide receiver on a football team at the Boys Club in Dothan and believed I was quite the polished receiver to be 9 years old. I convinced the teenage son of my father's friend to throw footballs to me in the street so that I could run patterns in front of the Bear's house. I was just sure that the Bear would look out his window and see this budding star receiver whom he would probably want to start recruiting at an early age to get a leg up on Shug Jordan at Auburn. We threw the ball until finally the neighbor's son's arm had given out. Quite dejected, I went to their house and realized I was not going to get to meet the Bear.

As the weeks passed following my performance of a lifetime, I awaited the call from my dad's friend to tell me how the Bear was searching for that tremendous mystery receiver he saw catching passes in the front yard. The call was never made; however, the magic of the whole experience did what my father hoped it would. I was hooked and have since been a life long fan of the Crimson Tide.

Andy Martin
Birmingham, Alabama

Denny Chimes
By Robert Hendrickson
Master of Art from the University of Alabama

Jim Lovette, Head Coach of the Fairfield Tigers

*"The doors opened and as I started to enter a huge
figure covered the back wall of the elevator...
It was the MAN! Coach Bryant in the flesh!
He had his hand stuck out and said, 'Hi Coach.
How's practice going?'"*

*– Jim Lovette*

# WILL I EVER
# MEET THE BEAR?

To say that I grew up an Alabama fan may be a bit of a stretch, but to say I grew up a fan of Coach Bryant is definitely accurate. My father was in the Air Force, and I did a lot of moving around in my early years. There were two things that remained constant in my life – my love for playing sports and playing them with the much older guys on the courts and fields of the Air Force base. When it came time to enter high school, I settled down in Red Bay, Alabama and lived with my grandparents so I could have some stability through these years. I truly became a fan of the Tide in high school and mainly because of Coach Bryant. My dad had coached, and I knew early on that coaching was going to be my vocation. So naturally, I wanted to play for and learn from the best – Coach Bryant.

I was not recruited by many big schools, but Mississippi State told me they were going to sign me and since no one else showed much interest, I was planning to attend school there, and at least, maybe play against a Coach Bryant team. However, an injury my senior year caused State to back off from recruiting me, and my high school coach turned his attention to getting me interviews with coaches in Division I programs. My coach made an appointment with the University of Alabama because he thought I could play there. I was scheduled to meet with Coach Bryant, and I couldn't believe the day had arrived that I was going to meet the MAN!

We traveled to T-town, and I remember being so excited I couldn't sleep at all the night before. What was I going to say to this living legend? How was I going to convince him that I would do whatever it took to be on the sidelines at Alabama and that even if I didn't play a down, I wanted to learn from the best?

The time finally came – I was not only going to meet the Bear, but I was also going to be interviewed by him, maybe even get a chance to play on his team. We entered the coaching offices with high expectations. We got to Coach Bryant's office only to find out that Coach Bryant had gotten sick and would not be able to meet with us, so the other coaches would talk to us. Unfortunately, they did not show much interest in me and really didn't give me the time of day. I can't say that I blame them because I played QB at a whopping 5'8" and 165 pounds and was not blessed with amazing speed.

Ironically, I learned later in my career that had Coach Bryant been there, I would have had a better shot at playing for the Tide. You see, he could simply look at you and talk to you and instantly know if you deserved a chance to play on one of his teams. In other words, he cared more about a player's heart and desire than how athletic he looked.

I went on to play football and baseball at Samford University in Birmingham, Alabama. While I was disappointed that I didn't end up at Alabama or a bigger program, I wouldn't trade anything for my experiences at Samford. The years at SU and the coaches and professors by whom I was blessed to be mentored solidified my dream of becoming a coach. Upon graduation at Samford, I entered graduate school at UA to get my masters in education with a focus in HPR (health, physical education and recreation).

I spent all my free time at the coaches' offices as I was now coaching in high school and wanted to gain as much knowledge as possible from the people who worked for Coach Bryant. I wore Steve Sloan out with questions, and he was always willing to share his experiences and philosophies, but I still never met Coach Bryant while getting my masters.

It was 1975, and I was now was the head coach at Fairfield High School in Birmingham. I had the honor of being selected to coach in the North-South All-Star Game and would head back to Tuscaloosa to lead the North team. It was the summer of 1975 and high school all-stars from the south and the north were beginning to arrive in Tuscaloosa to begin a week of practice. I was responsible for the North team as well as putting in the offense for the game. We used the locker rooms and practice fields that the Alabama team used, and you could see the excitement on the young players' faces as they walked through the halls of the Coach Bryant-led teams. I didn't let it show, but I was just as excited to walk down these same halls and coach on these same fields. The coaches' offices were on the third floor from where the locker rooms were, and we would have to take the elevator up to these offices.

After a couple of days of practice, things were not going exactly as I had planned. I was frustrated and tired as we had been practicing two and three times a day. I decided I could use some advice, so I went to the elevator to go up to talk to some of the Alabama coaches. I pushed the button for the elevator and waited with my head down still thinking about practice. The doors opened, and as I started to enter, a huge figure covered the back wall of the elevator... It was the MAN! Coach Bryant in the flesh! He stuck out his hand and said, "Hi Coach. How's practice going?" The silence was deafening and must have lasted an eternity. There I was... in front of the man with whom I was supposed to interview in high school... in front of the man I so desperately wanted to learn from while I was getting my masters degree, and I was frozen, speechless, and in total awe.

I eventually said something, but it was not earth shattering, and I can't say I remember it. I had gone over this meeting a thousand times in my head since high school, and now that I had a chance to say something to him, I blew it. I wonder to this day if I could have come up with something profound to say to Coach Bryant, but I doubt he would have rushed upstairs to write it down for future use. It's amazing how a couple of minutes almost 30 years ago can stay with you for the rest of your life and how much the years leading up to that encounter shaped my life. I left the elevator that day just hoping I would have the chance to have a fraction of the impact on young men's lives that Coach Bryant had on me.

Jim Lovette, '74
Red Bay, Alabama

Jim Lovette, Samford University
Best Offensive Back 1965, '66, '67, '68
All-American 1967

*"As I stood watching a roll of paper fall from the balcony above, my eyes read the scoreboard "34-7" and I knew we were Orange Bowl bound."*

*– Barney Duncan*

# TALES FROM
# THE TRUNK

As I checked my shirt pocket for the fourth time to secure my Orange Bowl tickets, I took a deep breath and prepared for the long drive south. This was not like any other drive to Miami. I imagined the thousands of other fans around the country starting the same trek, all of us hoping to drive home more victorious than when we left. Traveling from Chattanooga, Tennessee to Miami, Florida with my wife was a venture I will never forget. A few hours after leaving Chattanooga, we approached the Georgia Dome and remembered the SEC championship game we recently attended.

Mike DuBose's Crimson Tide had already gone into the swamp to defeat Steve Spurrier's powerful Florida Gators earlier in the year in an overtime thriller. Not only had Alabama defeated the Gators during the regular season, but again Bama proved their worth by beating the Gators for the SEC championship game. As I stood watching a roll of paper fall from the balcony above, my eyes read the scoreboard "34-7" and I knew we were Orange Bowl bound.

As the sun set, we greeted other Alabama fans with frequent honks and gradually felt the Bama family drawing closer to our tailgating site. Soon however, the talk turned from game time to gallons of stored water, generators, food, supplies, batteries and other resources the public was frantically stockpiling. While most people were preparing for the new millennium to roll in, my mind anticipated the Tide rolling in.

Later in the night, we drove down a long stretch of barren interstate. There were no other cars in sight as midnight approached. My wife and I celebrated the New Year alone as I flashed my lights and blew my horn for our own amusement. After a few minutes, bright lights and a honking horn approached from the northbound lane. We welcomed him into the new millennium, secretly wondering if the stadium lights would work.

The town was asleep as we finally arrived at Pro-Player Stadium at 4 a.m. Hardly able to control our excitement over the next 19 hours, we decided to take a walk along beautiful Miami Beach. Tropical birds sang a welcome for us while we anticipated welcoming the rest of the BAMA family in a matter of hours. At last, it was time for lunch at the sports bar packed with Michigan and Alabama chanting, "Roll Tide" and "Go Blue."

As game-time approached, we watched our team buses roll in. We rushed to the sidewalk to greet the players with shaking pompoms and waving pendants. My heart raced as I heard the players chant "Roll Tide" as they walked from the bus to the stadium. After welcoming the players to their new turf, we settled in to our traditional tailgating posture: a BBQ sandwich in one hand and a cold beverage in the other.

Finally, game-time arrived and we were thrilled when Alabama gained a 14-point advantage. But as luck would have it, the Maize and Blue came back and caught us by surprise which led to a tense final few minutes. With the game tied, Michigan drove the length of the field for a game-winning field goal attempt. Three young men in their early twenties got up to leave as the Wolverines set up the last play of the game. I caught one of the guys by the tail of the shirt and asked, "Don't you know that Alabama is famous for blocking kicks?"

Shaking off my grip, the young man started to descend the steps. But as the ball was snapped and the attempt was blocked, I caught a glimpse of the young man's smile and heard him scream, "How did you know? How did you know?' The answer was simple... I knew from a lifetime of watching Alabama football.

The game moved into overtime and Michigan delivered a quick touchdown. Alabama answered with a dramatic touchdown and we thought we were heading into our second overtime. Unfortunately, the extra point attempt sailed right and my heart sank knowing we had come so close. In the end, my pride was still overflowing, assured the Crimson Tide would continue to roll into a new millennium with many bowl games yet to be won.

Barney Duncan
Cedar Bluff, Alabama

Lindsay Lee and Shaud Williams

*"I still have my shirt with, 'Ready to Dominate the Dome' splashed across the front. That was my first SEC championship game with the Tide… but I know in my heart that it won't be the last."*

*– Lindsay Lee*

# GROWING UP
# WITH THE TIDE

I 'm 16 years old, but I've been raised by the Tide, and my roots go much farther back than my 16 years. Even though I was not fortunate enough to see Coach Bryant in person, most would say my Bama opportunities and experiences far exceed most girls my age… and probably many men twice my age!

I can remember as far back as the age of five when my family and I would gather together at my aunt's house on Saturdays to watch the Tide dominate whomever they were playing that week. Over the years, I had a chance to spend some time with Shaud Williams, and I was even lucky enough to be interviewed by Chris Sign of ABC 33/40 while visiting Elmwood Cemetery to pay my respects to Paul W. "Bear" Bryant on January 26, 2003 – the 20th anniversary of his death. But one of my fondest memories happened in 1999, when my "obsession" as some like to call it, was at an all time high.

I was a 12-year-old-girl with a love for the University of Alabama well beyond the comprehension of many of my classmates. My father, Len Lee, and I were lucky enough to have two tickets to the SEC Championship in Atlanta where Alabama was to take on Florida. My dad and I were driving along, almost to our hotel in Atlanta, when all of the sudden a state trooper flies in front of us, blocking all entrances to the interstate. Confusingly looking at my father, then back to the policeman, the trooper waved us through after two giant "ADVENTURE" buses maneuvered past. I looked in the rear view mirror and there were two buses behind us as well. These four buses, two in front and two behind, carried my "guys."

We followed the players right in, just like we were part of the team. We got our bags out of the trunk and hurried through the revolving doors in front of the hotel. When we got in, I looked straight up at all the linemen who were in the hotel with us. I looked behind me and noticed a somewhat smaller man. I looked at my dad who smiled and said, "How's the ankle, Drew?"

Andrew Zow lifted his head, smiled and said, "Fine. Thank you, sir."

It was all that I could do to keep my jaw from hitting the floor. And that was just the beginning!

We checked in and headed to our rooms. As we approached the top of the escalator, I noticed someone standing in the lobby alone listening to his headphones, like many players often do. My dad grabbed me by the hand and took me over to him. "Excuse me, Shaun... my daughter and I just wanted to shake your hand."

That was the day I first met one of the greats – Shaun Alexander. Looking back it almost seems like the whole experience was just a dream.

Not believing the people I was getting to meet, we climbed into the elevator. I looked next to me, and there he was... the voice of the Tide – Eli Gold. By then, I had purchased a game program and almost shaking, asked him to please autograph it for me. The man next to him turned out to be Kenny "Snake" Stabler, who also gave me an autograph.

My dad and I finally got up to our room and put all of our luggage down. Saleem Rasheed, who had become a family friend, asked my dad and me to meet him down in the lobby, so of course, we headed back out to the elevator to go down and meet him. As we got off the elevator, I saw a face that I never thought I'd get to see up close. "Nice to meet you, Coach Dubose," were some of the greatest words I have ever gotten to say.

We got to hang out in the lobby for a little while with Saleem and his brother, Dawud. Saleem introduced us to many other Bama players such as Kindal Moorehead, Reggie Grimes, Ryan Pflugner and Patrick Morgan.

That night, we rode to the Georgia Dome, our car adorned with our crimson Bama flags, the fight song playing on the stereo, and a victory in our hearts. As I watched the Tide whoop the Gators 34-7, I knew I was experiencing something special – coming in the underdog, and going out with your 21st SEC title. As you can imagine, that was one day in my life I will never forget. I still have my shirt with, "Ready to Dominate the Dome" splashed across the front. That was my first SEC championship game with the Tide... but I know in my heart that it won't be the last.

Lindsay Lee
Birmingham, Alabama

The Bama King – James Roberson

"*I carried a sign that said, 'I will Quarterback for Donuts.' Since all of our quarterbacks were banged up, I thought it was a clever sign. Little did I know how much attention I was going to get that Saturday. I bet I had my picture taken 100 times, plus I was featured in just about every highlight reel on TV.*"

*– James Roberson*

# THE BAMA KING

I have been a Bama fan for as long as I can remember, and following the Tide has been a fun journey to say the least. One event I look forward to each year is the traditional trip to Tuscaloosa for homecoming. I decorate my vehicle the night before the game with various slogans of encouragement for the Tide. My wife Sandra, and our friends David and Marcy Walton, and I always get up early and head out on Saturday morning. We always stop in Bucksville (between Bessemer and Tuscaloosa) at the Iron Skillet for breakfast, then rush on down to campus to claim our favorite tailgating spot. However, the real highlight is my costume for the homecoming parade and the game.

My homecoming costume has always been something unique, maybe an alien, a gorilla boy or super redneck, but since 2001, I have been Elvis, "The Bama King." In addition to my "King" costume, I always carry a sign that seems to gain attention. In 2001, the sign read, "Undercover NCAA Investigator." In 2002, "Put Me in Coach." But 2003 was my crowning slogan by far.

I found a fat Elvis suit with all the padding to make me look like I hadn't missed a meal in years. It was the white silk jumpsuit with gold trim, and, of course, the standard Elvis black hair and dark glasses. I carried a sign that said, "I will Quarterback for Donuts." Since all of our quarterbacks were banged up, I thought it was a clever sign. Little did I know how much attention I was going to get that Saturday. I bet I had my picture taken 100 times, plus I was featured in just about every highlight reel on TV. There I would be, holding my sign and cheering for my beloved Crimson Tide. The biggest thrill was that The Tuscaloosa News was doing a pictorial on homecoming faces in the crowd. They asked for my photograph and said I may be chosen as one of their featured pictures.

I went under the stadium at a predetermined place and time and had a portrait picture made. I drove back to Tuscaloosa County on Sunday from my home in Hueytown to buy a paper to see if I had made "the cut" – Low and behold – there I was in all my fatness, holding my sign and my tickets under the caption "Elvis Man and Bama Fan." I was elated. I bought all the papers in the machine. When I returned home, I scanned the picture into my computer and now use it for my wallpaper on my desktop. I also ended up as the featured picture on a Bama web site. Needless to say, I was the topic of conversation for days among my co-workers, church and family.

I can't wait until next year to see what "The King" will come up with next. I guess I might be considered outlandish, but I just love to see people smile, and being Elvis certainly breaks the ice. It gives me the opportunity to meet a lot of new people and share a good time. I am able to share the news that, as a Christian, there is no commandment saying "Thou Shall Not Commit Fun."

As a postscript to this story, my sign netted me so many donuts that Saturday that my entourage (that would be my friend Dave) had trouble carrying all the darn things. To all the Bama faithful – be on the lookout for me in the years to come, and "Thank ya, thank ya very much."

James Roberson
Hueytown, Alabama

Photo submitted by Linda Huffman

Lane Bearden, Danny Hill, Linda Huffman and Tyler Watts

Gene Stutts and Family
L-R – Britton (son), Evelyn (wife), Phillip (son) and Gene

*"There was now approximately one minute and 10 seconds left in the game, and the big question at that point was whether Alabama would go for two or kick the extra point. One Patrick Fain Dye, Alabama Assistant Coach at that time, convinced Coach Bryant to kick the extra point, and the score was now tied at 10."*

*– Eugene Stutts*

# OH HAPPY DAY!

I t was October 21, 1972, the third week in October, and that can only mean one thing – The Crimson Tide was playing the Big Orange, and the game that year happened to be at Rocky Top. My good friend, Billy Hulsey, and I were flying to Knoxville for the game, and we were afforded gorgeous blue skies for the trip. On the way to the airport, Billy and I discussed the important aspects of the game, especially the fact that Alabama was a six and a half point favorite. Before landing in Knoxville, I decided it would be in my best interest to make a friendly wager on the Tide. Oh, how right I was!

Unfortunately, for almost four entire quarters, the Tide failed to show up as Tennessee literally took Alabama to the wood shed. After three quarters of play, the score was 10-0 in Tennessee's favor. Uncharacteristically, Alabama had made only a couple of first downs, and to the best of my memory, had not crossed mid-field; however, midway through the fourth quarter, Bama was finally able to put three points on the board by way of a field goal, making the score 10-3.

With about two minutes to go in the game, Tennessee punted to Alabama giving Bama the ball at approximately mid-field. On the first or second play from scrimmage, Alabama fullback, Steve Bisceglia, broke one up the middle, sprinting 49 yards to the Volunteer two yard line. From there, Wilbur Jackson powered in for the touchdown, making the score 10-9. There was now approximately one minute and 10 seconds left in the game, and the big question at that point was whether Alabama would go for two or kick the extra point. One Patrick Fain Dye, Alabama Assistant Coach at that time, convinced Coach Bryant to kick the extra point, and the score was now tied at 10.

Alabama then kicked off to Tennessee and the ball went into the endzone, giving Tennessee possession on its own 20 yard line. On the first play from scrimmage, Tennessee quarterback Conridge Holloway, rolled out on a keeper and suddenly received a brutal lick by the Alabama defense. Miraculously, the ball spurted up in the air and was recovered by Alabama defensive end John Mitchell. It was now first and 10 for Alabama on the Tennessee 20 yard line. On the first play from scrimmage, Terry Davis, the Alabama wishbone quarterback, rolled out on a triple option keeping it up the middle for a score. Alabama then kicked the extra point, making the final score Alabama 17 - Tennessee 10. Incredibly, we had somehow not only beaten the Vols, we had also won by a touchdown. OH HAPPY DAY!

Eugene P. Stutts '64 & '67
Mountain Brook, Alabama

Photo submitted by Elise Stanfield

ROTC parade through Tuscaloosa 1933

Ray Massey having a cigar on his porch in Tuscaloosa

*"In the late 1950's and early 60's Shorty attended and made himself seen and known at every home game, including Legion Field, ran for Governor of Alabama in every governor's race and contributed more than his share to the profits of the spirits industry."*

*– Rayford Massey*

# SHORTY PRICE

No book about the Tide would be complete without the mention of Shorty Price. Shorty loved the Crimson Tide, politics and John Barleycorn in just about that order. In the late 1950's and early 60's, Shorty attended and made himself seen and known at every home game, including Legion Field, ran for Governor of Alabama in every governor's race, and contributed more than his share to the profits of the spirits industry.

Whether the Tide was winning or losing, Shorty always cheered them on. In those days, both in Legion Field and Denny Stadium, one could walk at field level in front of the student and fan sections. By the end of the first quarter, Shorty, properly infused and enthused, wearing his hat, tie and coat began his walk in front of the crowd in this area waving his arms, cheering the Tide, and jeering the opposition. Shorty's antics were special for the Tide-Auburn game. He always appeared carrying a stuffed tiger by the tail. As the game progressed, he would beat the stuffed tiger against the front of the stands, throw it, and finally jump up and down on it.

Win, lose or draw Shorty provided the lightness and humor that made you realize that football and politics were only a game and there would be another game next year and another election in four.

We could sure use you today, Shorty.

C. Rayford Massey '62 & '88
Knoxville, Tennessee

Britt Thames, Al Blanton and Jordan Baird

*I remember going to bed one night and praying for five of Alabama's players. I asked God to watch over them, give them the ability to make plays and help them to be winners. The next night I prayed for five more. The next night – five more. I continued to do this for a couple of weeks until I covered the whole team.*

*– Al Davis Blanton*

# A PRAYER FOR THE TIDE

I have been an Alabama fan for as long as I can remember. I guess it's similar to church – sometimes you don't really choose who to be for – you just are. For me, there was no moment of conversion. I was born into an Alabama family, and for that I'm thankful to this day. In fact, I learned something about the power of prayer from a special football season in 1992.

I was 14 years old when the '92 season began. I had a feeling that something special might happen because it was Alabama's 100th year of football. I had been through a lot as a fan, even at 14. I watched Auburn defeat Alabama four years in a row, and in '91 I witnessed a 35-0 pounding by Florida. Needless to say, I was a little skeptical about the upcoming season.

I knew we had a great defense and it would be hard for teams to score on us. As the '92 season rolled on, I began to believe Alabama might win the national championship. Although we had some close games, we just kept winning. I was so nervous before the SEC Championship game against Florida. I knew Shane Matthews was a great quarterback, and I also knew it would be difficult for us to stop their receivers.

That day in 1992 was probably the coldest I can remember. I remember celebrating with my best friend and strangers sitting next to us as Antonio Langham crossed the goal line for the winning score.

After the game, the media moguls had brought up the issue about whether Alabama should play for the National Championship. Some commentators said Florida State should jump us in the polls because we didn't have many flashy wins. I could not believe that, after all these years of waiting, I may not get to see us play for the National Championship. Fortunately, the voters felt we deserved it more than Florida State, and the rest is history.

I knew Alabama had a good team that year, but Miami was scary as they were the undefeated, defending National Champions. They had a Heisman trophy-winning quarterback and a corps of receivers that were among the best in the country. And they were Miami.

As the game approached, I became more and more worried about Miami. I listened to sports talk shows and read about the team we were up against. I wanted to do something about it, but I knew I had no control over the outcome of the game. The only thing I knew I could do was pray.

I remember going to bed one night and praying for five of Alabama's players. I asked God to watch over them, give them the ability to make plays and help them to be winners. The next night I prayed for five more. The next night – five more. I continued to do this for a couple of weeks until I covered the whole team.

I remember being in Tuscaloosa about a week before the game. I was in University Mall, and happened to run into Bama players Antonio Langham and Dameian Jefferies. I recognized them, and for some reason, I decided to go up and introduce myself. I walked up to Dameian and said, "I just want you to know that I'm praying for you – I'm praying for you to beat Miami." He gave a coy smile, then assured me that we would bring home a victory.

After the game, I thanked God for allowing us to beat Miami. I was overjoyed when we brought the national championship back to Alabama. In some way, I felt like I had helped. I felt like I was a part of the Alabama family, and felt like God had smiled upon us.

Al Davis Blanton '02
Birmingham, Alabama

Leo Cahalan, Kyle Cahalan, Lee Cahalan and John O'Rourke

*"Looking back, it's amazing how the simple choice of hats my dad made that November day affected my life in so many ways."*

*– Kyle Cahalan*

# THE GIFT OF A HAT

A simple choice of hats in a new hometown had a profound affect on my life. As a 7-year-old boy walking through Brookwood Village on a cold November day in Birmingham, I wandered into a store with my older brother, and it was filled with all kinds of sporting apparel. Being November, the entire front of the store was filled with Iron Bowl merchandise (half of it crimson and white, half of it orange and blue). We had recently moved to Alabama from Ohio a couple of months earlier, and the Iron Bowl didn't hold that much significance to us at that time. With the big game just one weekend away, my dad (a graduate of the University of Dayton in Dayton, Ohio) decided to buy my brother and me Alabama painter's caps (hey it was the 80s, and painter's caps were cool – I think).

In retrospect, my dad probably chose Alabama caps over Auburn caps merely due to the fact he had become an admirer of Coach Paul "Bear" Bryant by watching Alabama games on television over the years. According to my dad, only a couple of games were shown each weekend during his youth, and Alabama just so happened to be one of those teams televised more than a few times each year. Little did my dad know, but that simple choice of hats would cement my decision as to which in-state team my loyalty would lie, a decision that would affect my life in so many ways.

When I returned to school the next Monday, it was Iron Bowl week. Kids at school wore their team colors all week, and I wore the only piece of Iron Bowl merchandise I owned. For the first time I was an Alabama fan and proud of it. As the years continued, I have followed the Tide through thick and thin. When I approached the end of my junior year of high school, I knew I wanted to be an accountant, and my eyes wandered no further than the Capstone to pursue my degree. I finished graduate school in 1999 at The University and am married to my wonderful wife that I met while attending classes there.

Looking back, it's amazing how the simple choice of hats my dad made that November day affected my life in so many ways.

Kyle Cahalan '98
Birmingham, Alabama

Photo submitted by Damon McDonald

Inside Bryant-Denny Stadium

Spence, Sally, and Ann Winston Morano

*"We were within sight of Tutwiler Dorm when I heard the loudest, most awesome sound I had ever heard. It sounded like a cross between a tornado and a jet engine. The noise literally sent chills down my back, and I turned to my sister and asked, "What the hell was that?" She laughed and said, 'That was kickoff.'"*

*– Spence Morano*

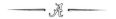

# THAT WAS KICKOFF

The year was 1992, and I was a high school junior in Richmond, Virginia, looking at colleges. My older sister, Sarah, had come to Alabama from Richmond on the suggestion of a lady who moved to Richmond from Mobile. Sarah loved the University of Alabama when she visited and became a freshman there in 1989. Little did I know then, but Sarah's decision to attend Alabama would later influence my choice of universities as well as the rest of my life.

For as long as I can remember, but especially during the years Sarah was in school, my family had always been Alabama football fans, definitely atypical for a family residing in Virginia. On Saturdays in the fall, we would unfortunately always get the boring, non-eventful, usually ACC, regional games on CBS and ABC. Fortunately, Alabama was always good enough to make it to a bowl game, and my family would literally anticipate for weeks watching our beloved Crimson Tide on T.V. With no ties to Alabama, I do not know exactly why my family members were such huge Bama fans, but like most folks, I guess we simply liked being associated with a winner.

As a high school junior, the two things I cared most about in life were football and girls, and The University of Alabama had both – in quantity and quality. It was during my junior year when I visited my sister in Tuscaloosa and finally got to see an Alabama game in person. Before that time, I had never been to a Division I college football game, and the people with whom I usually watched football rooted for UVA, not exactly a perennial powerhouse. On the day of my first UA game, I vividly recall walking from the Kappa Delta sorority house to the stadium. It was almost kickoff time, and I could not believe the number of people filing into the stadium. We were within sight of Tutwiler Dorm when I heard the loudest, most awesome sound I had ever heard. It sounded like a cross between a tornado and a jet engine. The noise literally sent chills down my back, and I turned to my sister and asked, "What the hell was that?"

She laughed and said, "That was kickoff."

I had never before heard the roar of "Roll Tide Roll," and when I did, I was so fired up, all I wanted to do was get into the stadium and see firsthand what Alabama football was all about. When we finally made it inside Bryant-Denny, I remember walking through a portal in the student section and seeing, to my sheer disbelief, 80,000 cheering fans, and I immediately knew this was the very best that college football had to offer. I was sold then and there. As best put these days by the stadium announcer: "This is Alabama Football." I was so taken by this indescribable spectacle that I did not even apply to other colleges. From that point forward, I was Bama Bound.

I became a freshman at The University in August 1994, and met my future wife, Sally Inzer, during the summer after my sophomore year. We dated throughout the remainder of my undergraduate studies and married after my first year at Cumberland Law School. We now have one daughter, Ann Winston, and live in Mountain Brook, Alabama. Without a doubt, it all began that hot Saturday afternoon when I heard the roar of "ROLL TIDE ROLL" for the first time. It truly changed my life.

Spence Morano '98
Birmingham, Alabama

Kylie Shannon and Dad

*"As we were making our way to the stadium, the Million Dollar Band was just outside, getting ready to march into Legion Field. ...As we went up to the band, they started marching and playing "Yea Alabama." I don't know what came over me at 5 years old, but I started marching right along with them."*

*– Kylie Shannon*

# "THIS IS FOR YOU DADDY…"

As a baby I was dressed in Tennessee booties and an Alabama jacket. My mom was a Tennessee fan and my dad pulled for Alabama. They wanted me to choose a team without them influencing my decision either way.

At the young age of five, I received my first live introduction to the University of Alabama. Knowing my mother had no interest in using the extra ticket, my dad took me to my first Alabama home game. I didn't know and probably didn't care who we were playing that day, but I was very concerned about when we would see the cheerleaders and when I'd hear the band play. As we were making our way to the stadium, I saw the Million Dollar Band getting ready to march into Legion Field. I was exploding with excitement to see the wonderful colors and hear the loud music. As we went up to the band, they started marching and began to play "Yea Alabama." I don't know what came over me at 5 years old, but I walked away from my dad, got in the middle of the band, and started marching right along with them. My dad walked along with us watching me. I paraded around so proudly, as if I was their newest member. When it was time to go to our gate, he took my hand and led me inside the stadium. I was smiling from ear to ear – my day had been made. I have been an Alabama fan ever since.

That's a story my dad loves to tell about me. Alabama football became a major father-daughter tradition for us. From the time I was just 5 years old even to now as an adult, I look forward to every Saturday in the fall and watching the Tide with my dad.

I have always enjoyed home games in Tuscaloosa the most. We park in the same spot every game. When I was a child, we would first walk to Tutwiler to eat (at what was then Julia's Café), and then we'd head to the bookstore to buy me a new shirt or some sort of Alabama memorabilia. Dad would take me to Sorority Row, then we would go meet his friends and co-workers at their motor home to tailgate before it was time to go to the stadium. But prior to each kick-off, I always loved to see the band march. The Million Dollar Band is still a game day highlight for me, even now that I'm older.

To my father's delight I decided to attend the University of Alabama. My mother was also very supportive of my decision. I spent four wonderful years at the University before graduating in 2000. My mother and I have made traditions of our own to enjoy with each other, and she even attends some home games, but Saturdays in the fall will always belong to my dad and me.

Kylie Shannon '00
Huntsville, Alabama

Little Kylie Shannon

Elise Renzetti with her dad, Ron Renzetti,
on her wedding day - May 21, 1994

*"My dad was a mere 5'6", which wasn't very tall,
however to me, my dad was a giant. All he had to
do was raise that one high arched, medium brown
eyebrow and I knew I had better get my rear in
gear and do what I was supposed to do."*

*— Elise Renzetti*

# J. R.²

As a kid, I remember the stories my dad, Joseph Ronald Renzetti, Jr., would tell about spending his childhood summers in Tuscaloosa with his cousins and how he was "the one" who brought the "Flat Top" hairdo back to Pennsylvania after his summer visit. I also remember thinking how cool it was that my granddad, Joseph Ronald Renzetti, liked to sign his name as "J.R.2." This was a clever little formula he created using his initials, J.R.R., while in Aeronautical Engineering School at The University of Alabama.

My pure blooded, Italian godfather – I mean grandfather – made his way deep into the south in the fall of 1933 after growing up in New York. Granddaddy had a dream of becoming an aeronautical engineer and the University of Alabama was one of the top four schools in the country at the time so the choice was clear.

From his photo album, his experiences were obviously enjoyable through those formidable years with his buddies at his dorm, Woods Hall. He documented many activities and landmarks around campus including a ROTC parade through downtown, Denny-Chimes and even a photo of George Denny – former school president and namesake of many familiar landmarks.

Sometime during his four years at The University Granddaddy met a Tuscaloosa native, Elizabeth Kirkland. Elizabeth, or Nana, as we called her, was born and raised in the small town of Cottondale, just outside Tuscaloosa. She had six sisters and one brother all of whom had lived in the Tuscaloosa area their entire life. Soon after graduating, my Granddaddy and Nana were married but Granddaddy soon realized he was not going to be able to utilize his education in Tuscaloosa and he began to search for a job elsewhere. After a few years of transferring around the country, they eventually wound up returning to the north and settling in the town of Ambler, Pennsylvania. Along the way came my Aunt Diane and almost three years later my dad, Joseph Ronald Renzetti, Jr., was born.

Over the years, I heard many stories of my dad's early days, all of which matched his somewhat curious and slightly rebellious tendencies. Many of the tales took place in Tuscaloosa where he inevitably spent most of his summers during childhood. Since my grandmother still had siblings in Tuscaloosa, my dad had plenty of aunts and uncles to stay with and plenty of first cousins to play with. One in particular that dad seemed closest with was his cousin, Buddy Kirkland, the son of my Great-Aunt Ruby. My dad spoke of walking down the dirt roads bare foot, going fishing in the pond, catching frogs at night, and doing many other activities in which typical little boys partake.

One of my favorite tales was how my Great Aunt Ruby got the grayish scar on her forehead. Either my dad or Buddy was trying to cast their fishing pole and hooked Aunt Ruby in the forehead. As I questioned my aunt, I later found out that apparently I made the whole fish hook thing up, but it was a good story anyway.

As the years went by and high school graduation approached, my dad chose to follow in his father's footsteps and attend the University of Alabama. Knowing my dad, I am certain he enjoyed a good time every now and then and that familiarity of surroundings definitely helped.

Legend has it that my dad, when he was a student at The University, had a little "get together" while my grandparents were on a trip to California. My grandparents were tipped off so they returned early, and my dad ended up working in the cafeteria for a semester. Again, I later found this story to be false, but for some reason, it has always stuck with me. Regardless whether fact or fiction, the stories I have heard did not make my dad out to be a saint; however, like many young college students, he did finally buckle down, graduate and go on to a very successful career with Xerox.

After marrying my mom, my brothers, Kevin and Tim, and I were born. Dad's job called for a couple of moves, and I spent the majority of my childhood years in the "Big Orange Country" of Knoxville, Tennessee. As you can imagine, this made our Bama family underdogs but we managed just fine.

My dad was a mere 5'6", which wasn't very tall, however to me, he was a giant. All he had to do was raise that one high arched, medium brown eyebrow and I knew I had better get my rear in gear and do what I was supposed to do. There are several things I remember about my dad, but my favorite and most vivid memories are when I felt like I really bonded and shared something special with him. One of those memories was sharing his love for Alabama football.

Before I even knew what college was, I remember the one big blue and gold ring on my dad's right ring finger. It seemed so huge to me, however, somewhat proportionate on dad's hands. It was his University of Alabama class ring. I always thought the blue sapphire, his birthstone, was an eyeball in the middle of all of the letters wrapped around it. I would sit on his lap and twist it around and around always begging for him to take it off—not a chance. Even though he took it off at night, he would religiously return this prize possession once morning arrived.

As I got a bit older, I realized football was the perfect opportunity to keep him company. Being the energetic man he was, Dad was not very attentive to me and considering my gender, female, and his "race", Italian, I always felt I had to vie for his attention. So as fall approached each year, I would begin to hear the football chatter among my dad and his peers. I would then know it was almost time to start learning "the lingo" once again. As gameday mornings arrived, I would go about my business until I heard the radio moving in and out from static to voices to static to music to static, until finally settling on some man's voice that to me was nobody, but to dad was obviously a very familiar and loved sound.

My dad had turned our medium stained, solid walnut Drexel dining room buffet into a regular ole stereo/entertainment center. The top drawer was just barely deep enough to hold the turn table and the bottom drawer is where the tuner fit perfectly. On each side of the drawers were little cabinets that held my mom and dad's record collection ranging from Pink Floyd to Neil Diamond and then, of course, Michael Jackson's first solo album, "Thriller". After the radio was settled into its permanent position for the next several hours my dad and I would pretty much sit Indian style in the middle of our rather large and awkward living room.

Our house had a very open floor plan and I'm not sure if we just couldn't furnish the area properly or if it was a planning mistake and really should have been an entrance parlor, but instead ended up being an odd looking over extension of our living room. However, I must say the area made for a great Hot Wheels track in the carpet and, of course, great space for our Christmas tree, and plenty of room for Santa, but best of all, a very large yet cozy place for Dad and me to listen to some stranger get very excited about football. This went on for years. It was very exciting for me to share these Saturdays

Joseph Ronald Renzetti, Sr.

even though I had no clue who any of the players were and could not for the life of me visualize what in the world was going on during each play. It was all just a bunch of words crammed together that made absolutely no sense to me. The only thing that really mattered was the thrill of watching my dad sit, then stand, then grumble, then sit, then clap, then cheer, and so on.

Usually around half time, he would either get up or start dinner, or my favorite, he would go make sandwiches. He always made the best. He would start making them then ask if I wanted one. I would say no, and then he would bring his scrumptious looking, piled high delicatessen, and of course, my tummy would start to rumble. You could see the flames come out of his ears when I would say so sweetly, "Daddy, I changed my mind. Will you make me one too?" After everything was already put away, he would usually tell me to go and get it myself, and my usual reply was, "Yeah, but daddy you make them so much better." He sometimes would give in after seeing my poor puppy dog blue eyes and give me his sandwich and go make himself another. My dad had a strange way of showing love, but on Saturdays, I just knew.

As time went by and we became older, those Saturdays grew further apart, but whenever given the opportunity to be together on a rare Saturday, it always seemed to pick up as if we had never missed a beat. I don't think my dad ever knew my purpose behind those Saturdays, and I'm not sure I realized how important they were until those Saturdays were no more.

Elise Renzetti
Birmingham, Alabama

Joseph Ronald Renzetti, Sr. with his
bridge built as an engineering project.

Brad Pickering, Mark Huffman and Jimmy Campbell

*"I gave this large man a cursory scowl with a peripheral glance. But that glance turned my anger into confusion. Though I'll never know for sure, I thought I was standing next to 'The Biscuit' himself, Cornelius Bennett."*

*– Brad Pickering*

# RUBBING ELBOWS

I t was my first football season since graduating from the University of Alabama. I was excited about the big weekend back in Tuscaloosa. I knew that I would be visiting old friends and running into some familiar faces, but I just didn't realize how familiar.

I got off of work early that Friday, met up with my friends and made the journey to Tuscaloosa. Our first stop was Gallette's for "Happy Hour." This also included a free Juke Box and Gallette's burgers (which are absolutely amazing if you haven't tried them). It's the cheap man's way to get prepped for a football weekend!

As the evening progressed, we took a while to tour The Strip. We went to the new places and the old. We wanted to see how everything had changed since we had left there. It is amazing how much can change in a few short months. Now, six years later, some of it is hardly recognizable.

By the end of the night, we arrived at The Booth. This is where things would get interesting and perplexing. My friends and I shared stories of the great games, the tough professors, the beautiful co-eds, and the benefits of college life as compared to our new careers. As we visited and commemorated our glorious days at the Capstone, nature called. I made my way to that sanctuary of relief, and I noticed the long line that I would have to endure. When I finally arrived, I was reminded of the simple contraption that must have been there for 100 years. Most guys will instantly recognize the word "trough," and to those who have visited this establishment, I'm sure some of you can remember the facilities that were in there years ago—an old trough in a room that was too tight for one guy, much less two. Late in the evening, guys would develop an expeditious system of going in two at a time. On the night in question, I had just made it in and attempted to uphold the unspoken etiquette of avoiding any contact with the stranger standing about one inch away. While trying to concentrate, I heard someone outside say that the bathroom was full. Nevertheless, the door opened and a large man pushed his way between us. The code of etiquette had been broken. What an outrage! Trying to uphold this unspoken code, I gave this large man a cursory scowl with a peripheral glance. But that glance turned my anger into confusion. Though I'll never know for sure, I thought I was standing next to the 'Biscuit' himself, Cornelius Bennett.

I had always been a huge fan of Cornelius Bennett from his playing days at The University through his successful pro career. In an instant, I remembered the plays, the wins, and all of the things that made him one of my favorite players of all time and a football legend. And there I stood, literally rubbing elbows with him (or so I thought). What could I have done? I couldn't introduce myself and shake hands. It wouldn't have been appropriate to ask for an autograph. A pat on the back with thanks for the memories wouldn't have worked either. And then I thought to myself, "What if I am wrong? How embarrassing would that be?" So I just stood there totally distracted from my original purpose, wondering what to do and whether or not it was even him. While I pondered, he exited that confined room and I didn't see him again.

All in all, we had a great weekend back in Tuscaloosa. The trough incident is one that I'll never forget and a story that I'll probably tell for years. I still wonder from time to time if I'll ever get to meet Cornelius 'The Biscuit' Bennett. Needless to say, I hope to get that opportunity under better circumstances.

Brad Pickering '98
Birmingham, Alabama

*"I was so hopeful and fired up that I believe Kitchens could have passed the ball to me and I could have destroyed that Auburn defensive curtain. Instead, Freddie tossed a swing pass to Dennis Riddle, and he seemed to effortlessly dance into the end zone for the game-winning touchdown!"*

*– Vance Ballard*

—— $\mathcal{A}$ ——

# PART OF THE GAME

D ear Tide Faithful... It was nightfall, and you would have never convinced me that the guys on the field were more tired than I was. The band was pumpin' the air with crimson notes of grit and gut check. The noise was deafening, and the chants pounded in your chest like a subwoofer. I felt so small as I gazed around at an ocean of frenzied excitement.

We had been cheering all game, literally! I was a cheerleader, and we had just a few ticks left on the clock. The Tide had marched relentlessly down the field, and the only thing between us and the goal line was 11 orange and blue jerseys.

All cheering was put aside and although we were cheerleaders in uniform, we were just regular fans at this point, holding our breath and praying to God for a break....and a touchdown!

I turned and grabbed a megaphone...I don't know what hit me, but I turned on the crowd like a rabid dog and started slowly yelling that familiar "Roll Tide!" Well, it caught. What a feeling, to know that you started it with a few people at first...then a few more and then four or five chants into it, the whole stadium was taunting "Roll Tide!"

I was so hopeful and fired up that I believe Kitchens could have passed the ball to me and I could have destroyed that Auburn defensive curtain. Instead, Freddie tossed a swing pass to Dennis Riddle, and he seemed to effortlessly dance into the end zone for the game-winning touchdown. We went absolutely crazy...it was pandemonium on the sidelines, just like it was in the stands.

Riddle circled around, and we bumped chests as if I had his respect and he recognized me as having helped him pull it out. I felt like a champion, and so did everyone else. It was a little moment for him, but that single act of acknowledgment meant the world to me.

Alabama beat Auburn that year at Legion Field, and that was the last time I ever cheered an Alabama-Auburn game. It's a good thing, because I'm not sure my crimson heart could endure another nail biter of that magnitude.

I ended up snatching a game ball from the field and went into the locker room after the game. I got Dennis Riddle and Coach Gene Stallings to sign the ball. That ball sits in a box in my office today. I refer to that precious piece of memorabilia as proof that I got to live a Bama dream, and I will cherish that experience forever...the time I thought I helped the Tide beat the Tigers!

Roll Tide now and forever!

Vance Ballard '00
Birmingham, Alabama

Photo submitted by Linda Huffman

Friendly Rivals
Diana Hanson and Jim Tucker with Inflatable Big Al

L-R: The Honorable Vincent J. Schilleci (UA Football Team, 1967-70, K [placekicker], UA C&BA 1972), Julie Schilleci-Foster (UA School of Communications 1999; UA Law 2002), and Greg Foster (UA C&BA 1995)

*"There, I remember eating barbeque and being able to grab a Coca-Cola out of a big plastic 30-gallon garbage can full of ice and drinks. For a fifth grader, it didn't get any better than this."*

*— Greg Foster*

# FINALLY SEEING IT IN PERSON

O f course, there are many Tide games that are memorable, but for me, the best memory I have is my first Alabama game to see in person.

Growing up in a small town in Alabama, my first connection to Alabama football was listening to the games on Saturdays while bailing hay. Later, I heard stories from my great aunt about the many exciting bowl games she had attended, and as a fifth grader at that time, I had always dreamed of going to Bryant-Denny Stadium and seeing a game in person.

At last, I got that opportunity when invited by my great aunt and uncle to be their guest at an upcoming game. When we arrived on campus, we went to the athletic booster house located on the cemetery side of Bryant-Denny. There, I remember eating barbeque and being able to grab a Coca-Cola out of a big plastic 30-gallon garbage can full of ice and drinks. For a fifth grader, it didn't get any better than this.

But it did. The game was awesome, and I had a stadium dog, much better than any hotdog I had ever eaten. As for the game, the afternoon was filled with utter excitement as the Tide prevailed in the end. I could not believe the noise and I was actually there seeing the greatest football program in the country battle on the gridiron. This sure beat listening to the games in the hot hay fields in Coaling, Alabama, and it had such a lasting effect on me that I was drawn to The

University eight years later as an incoming freshman where I experienced four of the greatest years of my life. Where else could I receive an excellent education and have a welcomed week ending distraction to share with family and friends?

For me, the answer was easy. Nowhere.

Greg Foster '95
Birmingham, Alabama

# SWAMP MEAT

The term "road trip" as applied to most American households involves a great deal of thought, planning, and attention to detail. But as many of you know, the term "road trip" takes on a whole new meaning for the typical twenty-one year old college student. In that scenario, the decision is usually made when a group of four to six loudmouths get together after a number of adult beverages, coupled with utter boredom from the day's events.

The University of Alabama was scheduled to play the Florida Gators in Gainesville on October 2, 1999. The Tide had suffered a heartbreaking loss to Louisiana Tech two weeks before, and third-ranked Florida was a heavy favorite in the game. Nevertheless, a group of friends and I decided to load up and travel to Gainesville for the weekend.

It started out as a small group of four, but a Thursday night out at Gallette's, a famous Tuscaloosa watering hole, produced a few more verbal commitments. When Friday morning rolled around, 10 anxious guys were waiting at my house to leave to Gainesville. Due to the unexpected number of travelers, we had to find another vehicle to carry the load. After much thought and a number of different offers, a friend of mine volunteered his parents' 1985 Chevy Impala, sport package style.

Packed like sardines in the Impala and a Grand Cherokee, we embarked on our journey to the Sunshine State.

Surprisingly, there were no mishaps on the way down, and we rolled into Gainesville around nine o'clock. Now, the houses in Gainesville are not your typical Southern style home. They are more like small beach houses that resemble condominiums – wicker tends to be the furniture of choice.

When we arrived, we noticed that there were an inadequate number of beds for 10 unexpected guests. Nevertheless, we unloaded our belongings, got dressed, and went out on the town. The Florida faithful were all decked in their floral beach attire, gel glistening in their hair to match the gold chains around their necks, and a tan that would make George Hamilton envious.

After a while, we began to inquire about their thoughts regarding the game. One over-confident Florida fan said, "Do you actually think you have a chance tomorrow?" I believe that he echoed the sentiments of most of the Florida students there that night.

We eventually made it back to our small bungalow and decided to crash for the night. Because there was not a great deal of room, most of us slept on the floor. My friend Dave got over zealous and made the kitchen counter home for the evening.

We awoke around 9:30, just in time to watch ESPN College Gameday. I realized then how nervous I was about the game when I found out that Florida hadn't lost at home since 1994. We arrived at the dreaded "Swamp" and took our seats in front of the Florida student section.

Surprisingly, Bama led at halftime 13-6, and the Florida students began to empty out of the stadium. Little did we know that the students were allowed to leave the game and come back, even after purchasing dollar beer and whiskey at a bar next door. When halftime ended, we were pelted continuously in the second half with plastic cups.

The third and fourth quarters were back and forth. Bama tied the game and forced overtime with a Shaun Alexander run from the 13 yard line. In overtime, Florida wasted no time scoring a touchdown, but kicker Jeff Chandler missed the extra point. On Bama's first play, Shaun Alexander tied the game with a 25-yard counter run around left end. After Chris Kemp's kick sailed left of the upright, our hearts collapsed. But we noticed that a yellow flag had fallen. Offsides Florida! Kemp's second attempt squeaked through the uprights for a 40-39 victory. Of course, a rousing rendition of "Rammer Jammer" cleared most of the Florida fans out of the Swamp, and we stayed long after the game to celebrate.

The next day we awoke to find the poor Impala victimized at the hands of a few local ruffians. The front windows had been smashed, and the steering column removed in a failed attempt at grand theft auto. We wondered if the Impala had somehow improved in its overall condition. We collectively put our heads together and somehow managed to hotwire the car with a pair of needle-nosed pillars and vice-grips.

So there we were, the 10 of us, heading north to Tuscaloosa with a Tide victory in a Cherokee and a beat up Chevy Impala.

Stuart Curry, '00 & '04
Birmingham, Alabama

Mark Huffman Tailgating

*"Although the 1992 Championship team was
considered to be defensive by nature; Alabama
managed over 260 yards on the ground. This
incredible dominance on the ground enabled
Derrick Lassic to win the Sugar Bowl MVP Award
with 135 yards rushing and two touchdowns."*

*– Mark Huffman*

158

———— ℋ ————

# TROPICAL DEPRESSION

"**M**iami will Blow away Alabama" "Miami is No.1. It will stay that way. Alabama doesn't have a hope, or a prayer, or a shot in the dark of upsetting the Hurricanes for the national championship in tonight's Sugar Bowl. And it won't even be close. Alabama will be trounced, clobbered, mauled, devastated, humiliated and left for dead. The Crimson Tide will not roll, not even a little bit. Tonight you will experience low Tide. Probably even ebb Tide. You won't even have to hike up your pant legs to wade in what will be left of this Tide after the Hurricanes pass through".

Michael Ventre of the Los Angeles Daily News wrote the above quote on January 1, 1993. Obviously, he did not understand Alabama Football.

As No.1 ranked Miami and No.2 ranked Alabama rolled into New Orleans for the 1993 Sugar Bowl, most of America seemed to agree with Mr. Ventre. That is, except for Gene Stallings and the Alabama Family. In the weeks leading up to the game, Coach Stallings continued to maintain that he did not feel like Alabama was an underdog. After 60 minutes of football, a courageous Alabama team proved the skeptics wrong.

Final score: Alabama 34, Miami 13

All season long, the nation's number one defense helped Alabama win games. This game was no different. Alabama's defensive front kept Miami's vaunted offense under check, allowing just 48 rushing yards. The Alabama secondary was equally effective, shutting down Gino Torretta and having one of the greatest plays in history involving defensive back George Teague. Losing by three touchdowns, Torretta connected with Lamar Thomas who was running down the sideline towards the end zone. Teague managed to run Thomas down from behind, strip the ball out of his hands, and reverse the field for an Alabama gain. Although the play was negated due to an Alabama offsides penalty, it goes down as one of the most memorable plays in bowl history. Although the 1992 Championship team was considered to be defensive by nature, Alabama managed over 260 yards on the ground. This incredible dominance on the ground enabled Derrick Lassic to win the Sugar Bowl MVP Award with 135 yards rushing and two touchdowns.

With this magnificent win, Alabama won its 12th National Championship…and the tradition continues.

As I think back to that magical game. I can only assume that Michael Ventre of the Los Angeles Daily News had been confused. As he found out, the mighty Hurricane he forecasted had quickly become an insignificant tropical depression. I hope he also learned that the mighty Tide will always Roll!

Mark Huffman '97
Birmingham, Alabama

Danny Hill, Jay Barker and Linda Huffman

Tony and Marie Brandino
The Aloha Bowl 1985
Alabama 24 – Southern California 3

*"Well, as Coach Bryant walked from the playing field and toward our dressing room, there was a series of thunderous ovations from the Nittany Lions' fans. Then, to the surprise of Alabama supporters, those wonderful folks formed a tunnel of sorts under the grandstands, six or eight people deep on both sides, and continued their cheering as he walked between them. I'll admit I felt a tear or two forming as I witnessed that stylish display."*

*– Tony Brandino*

# GLORIOUS
# HAPPY VALLEY

One of the more pleasant things I've seen while following University of Alabama football is a series of games with Penn State. It has allowed me to meet a lot of genuinely nice people and to develop a better appreciation for the Nittany Lions' program.

I sort of knew what to expect when we started playing on a more consistent basis, having attended the Liberty Bowl in 1959, but in many ways I was like most Alabama fans in my analysis. To put it kindly, I thought Penn State was a power in that part of the nation, something like an upper level Ivy League, and wouldn't have a prayer of winning in the Southeastern Conference. As for the Nittany Lions' fans, well, I surmised they were a bunch of crisp' talking folks who didn't know a thing about the Deep South and had little respect for the good people who live here.

All of that foolishness started changing on December 31, 1975, when Alabama defeated Penn State in the Sugar Bowl. By the time we played again in the 1979 Sugar Bowl, which we won 14-7, I had a grand appreciation for the Nittany Lions and their fans.

Classy, to the highest degree, is the way to describe them, far and away the most pleasant opposing fans I've encountered. Their supporters are gracious winners and gracious losers, which is the ultimate measuring stick. While most programs have bad bananas among their fans, Alabama included, I can truthfully say I haven't met one from Penn State.

We've met on the playing field 13 times, with Alabama winning eight and Penn State winning five, and it's a shame the Crimson Tide and Nittany Lions don't play every year.

A good example of classy behavior surfaced at State College, Pennsylvania on November 14, 1981, as Coach Paul "Bear" Bryant was attempting to break Amos Alonzo Stagg's all-time victory record. He was trying to secure Number 314 that afternoon, with number 315 being the ultimate goal, and we defeated Penn State, 31-16.

It was only the fourth time we'd played Penn State and I was anxious to see how their fans would react, especially since we'd won the previous two games, both by only seven points. Well, as Coach Bryant walked from the playing field and toward our dressing room, there was a series of thunderous ovations from the Nittany Lions' fans. Then, to the surprise of Alabama supporters, those wonderful folks formed a tunnel of sorts under the grandstands, six or eight people deep on both sides, and continued their cheering as he walked between them. I'll admit I felt a tear or two forming as I witnessed that stylish display.

Then as Marie and I were walking to the motor home, we were stopped time and again by Penn State fans. "Hey, sir, come have a beer with us." "How about a hot dog?" "Can we fix you a stiff drink to help you celebrate?" I'm telling you, by the time we got to the motor home I didn't care if we had won or lost. Gee, they're such super people.

-Excerpt from FANtastic by Tony Brandino

# THE LUCK STOPS HERE

At least that is what the T-shirts they were selling said the week before the game. It was 1986 and we were playing Notre Dame at Legion Field. I will never forget standing in line outside the student section three and a half hours before the game in order to get a seat as close to the 50-yard line as possible. What a great game – Cornelius "Biscuit" Bennett ripped up poor Steve Buerlein all day!

Roll Tide!

Amanda Brasher Black '89
Birmingham, Alabama

Photo submitted by Kelly Moore

Touchdown Jesus: Notre Dame vs. Alabama 1987
Notre Dame Campus - South Bend, Indiana

Photo submitted by Elise Renzetti

Paul "Bear" Bryant 1933

*"I don't know how others measure the mark of a great man, but it seems to me that someone who can pass through your life briefly, in the most casual way, and leave you with a feeling you will never forget, is unassailably a great man."*

*– Daphne Stephens*

# THE MAN

I don't know how others measure the mark of a great man, but it seems to me that someone who can pass through your life briefly in the most casual way and leave you with a feeling you will never forget is unassailably a great man. I met just such a man once. His name was Paul "Bear" Bryant.

I grew up in Franklin County, Tennessee. In case you don't remember your UT trivia, Franklin County was the home of both Johnny Majors and Phil Fulmer. Always the type that wasn't afraid to go against the crowd, I was a Bama fan. It wasn't always easy to be a Bama fan in Franklin County, surrounded by a whole nest of orange fanatics, but it kept football season interesting.

After high school, I moved to Chattanooga and attended college. In May of 1980, Bear Bryant came to Chattanooga, Tennessee, and through some business acquaintances of my sister, Paula, I got the opportunity to meet him. Paula was invited to a business party and knowing my love for football and Bama, she let me tag along. It was by all standards a small party attended by a few of Bear's friends and several business acquaintances.

At 21 years of age, I was awed to be in the same room with Bear Bryant. I spent several boring hours in the corner with my sister, but I don't think I ever took my eyes off the Bear. It seemed that if he was up, he was surrounded by the men, talking loudly, joking and listening to his every word. If he sat down, the crowd followed closely and blanketed his every move. As I watched this mobile mob, I remember noticing that Bear didn't appear to be too interested.

By a stroke of luck, at one point I realized he was sitting alone. Driven by a resolution to meet the Bear that was strong enough to overcome my shyness, I went over and introduced myself to him. I then started talking football, and I'm sure there's no need to remind anyone that football was a topic he loved to discuss.

A few minutes later, Bear was up telling football stories to the entire room. It was special to hear those stories straight from the legend's mouth and those personal stories he told that I haven't heard or read since really stand out in my mind. Everyone knows he was he a great football coach, but he was also a natural-born storyteller. He basked in the attention, and it was suddenly apparent he was a bit of a ham.

He stayed by my side for the remainder of the party, and I was having the time of my life. In addition to the football stories, he told me a little about his life outside of football. He shared a story about his early life, his experiences as a player and as a coach, and told me about his wife and children. Coach Bryant paid me a high compliment when he said I reminded him of his granddaughter in some ways. As the party drew to a close, he asked me if I would join him for breakfast the next morning.

When I arrived the following morning, it was his behavior at breakfast that left a standing impression on me. For a few seconds, I glimpsed at the man inside the Bear. As we prepared to eat, Coach Bryant asked if I would be offended if he offered thanks for the food. He simply stated that he had grown up poor and he never wanted to forget where his food came from. The words he spoke were simple, but the meaning and the feeling behind them said volumes. The greatest football coach of all time, a man of considerable wealth and fame, and a man who was a living legend humbled himself before his God to offer thanks for his food. Never have I felt so moved. Coach Bryant had touched my life.

Daphne Stephens
Chattanooga, Tennessee

Robert Hendrickson and his mom, Jean Hendrickson

*"I found myself at the 35-yard line and half way
up the stands for what would be the first ever
SEC Championship game in Birmingham,
Alabama. I couldn't believe we got tickets for
the game. I was so excited and so bundled up from
the cold I had trouble moving. I felt like
the "Stay Puft" Marshmallow Man or that
kid on A Christmas Story."*

*– Robert Hendrickson*

# MY BEAR

I found myself at the 35-yard line and half way up the stands for what would be the first ever SEC Championship game in Birmingham, Alabama. I couldn't believe we got tickets for the game. I was so excited and so bundled up from the cold I had trouble moving. I felt like the "Stay Puft" Marshmallow Man or that kid on A Christmas Story. As the Tide went through their warm up drills, I looked through the binoculars and picked out all the great players and coaches. Little did I know as the team ran onto the field, this game would hold my most vivid football memory and would mark the beginning of a personal legend.

Growing up, my family always talked about Bear Bryant as a football god, a genius of tactics and grit. Unfortunately, I only knew of his greatness from their stories and every so often watching an old game on ESPN Classic. Somehow, there was always something missing, an aura that I didn't sense, a greatness that I couldn't measure. I realized that while the special "something" Coach Bryant had would continue to be a driving force in the Alabama saga, I would always wonder what it was like to experience a game with the Bear on the sidelines or watch the "Bear Bryant Show" on Sundays. It was like there was a void in my Alabama experience because I didn't get to grow up with this legend. It was the way my mom's eyes lit up whenever I asked her about Coach Bryant or when my sisters cried the day that Bear died. I knew he was special but I would never have the opportunity to experience his legend like so many people were able to.

Coach Stallings had been there though, and he represented all of the qualities that Bear represented. Not to say that Coach Stallings was a mirror image of Coach Bryant, but he was as close as you could get to what my family had been describing all of these years and I loved the fact I could watch him lead us onto victory every Saturday. He had learned as an assistant under Coach Bryant until 1965 when we lost him to that agricultural school in Texas.

Speaking of agricultural schools, it was six years later that I made one of the worst decisions of my life and decided to attend the school down south. I foolishly thought Auburn had a better art program than Alabama and went there to get my degree. I was at school on the plains, but with the crimson force on my side and the will of Luke Skywalker, or Joe Willie, I refused to be seduced by the dark side. As a lifelong fan of The Tide, these four years would make me an even bigger fan due to the fact I was able to witness how the evil empire operated. It was especially torturous during football season as my studies and budget did not allow me to attend many Bama games. I would sit in my room at my apartment and watch Bama play every Saturday, even if I had to watch the scrambled pay-per-view games, while my roommate and his friends would celebrate another victory over some Division II school. The one highlight of my four years down there was that I was able to witness the first victory on The Plains in person. What made it even better was that my family had come to visit and attend the game, even though the ticket my sister bought me was in the last row of the upper deck. Afterwards, my apartment was full of celebrating Bama fans, and my roommate got to spend an evening in his room suffering. Payback is so sweet! Bama ended up winning the SEC Championship that year, and I proudly wore my crimson polo shirt, a uniform that the Tiger fan is not familiar with, and I enjoyed watching the agony on the face of every Auburn spawn. As much as I enjoyed snubbing those Tiger fans, I kept thinking about how I missed the days of going to watch games at Bryant-Denny and Legion Field, and watching Coach Stallings prowl the sidelines. I was fortunate enough to get a scholarship to Alabama to attend graduate school and am still attending school at this wonderful campus as I write this. While Coach Stallings is no longer on the sidelines, I often think back to the days when he was here and how he brought the program back to national prominence on and off the field.

So on a cold December night over a decade ago, a man who is almost the spittin' image of The Bear became my legend. I remember the game as a close one. I suppose my nails were just about gone by halftime, and as Antonio Langham intercepted and scored the winning touchdown, Legion Field erupted in a way I had never heard before. I wish I could measure the force that shook the stadium because I know it was bigger than the little earthquake they would supposedly measure in Death Valley. That was a crazy moment. Everyone with the exception of 10,000 people were screaming and somehow I was hugging strangers in the bleachers, something Mom would not have approved of on any other occasion.

That night Gene Stallings and the Tide had done the impossible–finish the season with an undefeated record of 12-0 and beat the mighty Florida Gators. It was a great feeling riding in the charter bus after the game and listening to Eli Gold recap the game. It was then that I realized Coach Stallings made me believe in the program again.

Gene Stallings had become my legend, my Bear.

Robert Hendrickson '04
Tuscaloosa, Alabama

# 17 TO 16 IS NO MORE

Growing up in Cullman, much like any other part of the state, kids were persuaded at an early age to make a choice – Alabama or Auburn. I remember in P.E. the teachers at my elementary school would divide us up for football games as Alabama against Auburn. It was 20 on 20 football. The female teacher was an Auburn fan and the male was an Alabama fan. We took the game very seriously, like the Omicron Delta Kappa - James E. Foy V Sportsmanship Trophy was on the line. (That's the official name of the Iron Bowl Trophy for those of you who didn't know.)

I remember how bad it hurt when Auburn won 17 to 16 and I had to go to school the following Monday. However, I also remember the next year Bama was back for revenge and won 35 to 0. The reason I can easily remember the score was because, as kids, we always had a rhyme and the rhyme that year was...

"17 to 16 is no more"
"35 to nothing is the score"

The school yard games trickled over into some pretty intense one-on-one football games in the yard with my brother. He was a huge Auburn fan so there was a serious rivalry. I remember that I was Johnny Musso going over the top or Terry Davis running the wishbone. He was maybe Pat Sullivan or some other Auburn player. We had a lot of fun pretending and neither of us likes to lose. Even though he was older and bigger, I was always determined to score on goal line stands.

After high school, my brother joined the Air force and moved to Florida and developed a pretty strong distaste for Gators. He said getting away from all the trash talking made it a little bit easier to pull for the Tide. He was visiting me during the '92 National Championship Game against Miami and was almost as excited as I was when we won. We both were jumping around like we were little kids again. This championship meant more to me because it was the first one I celebrated as an adult.

Even though my brother has softened and now pulls for the Tide except against Auburn, we still have a tradition that the loser has to call the winner after the Iron Bowl. We also don't like talking trash quite as much anymore since it can come back and bite you, but don't think for a second that when the big game is through, I am hoping that it is my phone that is ringing!

Ernie Dease
Birmingham, Alabama

Davis, Malia, Charlie and Emma Stewart

*"From a visual perspective, it appeared that
Miami fans were bound to a strange type of dress
code. ... The code itself was fairly limited in scope.
From what I could discern, the code mandated
that you could wear either a green, orange and
white jumpsuit that looked like something a crab
fisherman off the coast of Alaska wears to stay dry,
or they could go with a more traditional look
which simply involved a pair of jeans and/or sweat
pants and an untucked oversized Miami football
jersey, which had to be large enough to hang to the
person's knees."*

*– Charlie Stewart*

# A "BIG EASY" WIN

On December 30, 1992, my future wife, a group of friends, and I headed from Birmingham to New Orleans to celebrate New Year's Eve and attend the college football national championship game between the University of Alabama and the University of Miami. The entire season had already been a magical one for the Crimson Tide. We were undefeated, we had the number one defense in the country, and we were winners of the first ever SEC championship game. The Hurricanes were the defending national champions and were ranked number one in the country. The Superdome in New Orleans was the perfect setting to host such an event.

Naturally, we hit Bourbon Street on the night of our arrival, and it didn't take us long to realize that Miami fans possessed a strong desire to be noticed. Whether it was the apparel they chose to wear or just the loud obnoxious ringing of their voices, you couldn't walk down a street in New Orleans and not notice one of these people. From a visual perspective, it appeared that Miami fans were bound to a strange type of dress code. I don't know if the University of Miami itself instigated this code, but there was little doubt the code was universally adhered to by Miami fans. The code itself was fairly limited in scope. From what I could discern, the code mandated that you could wear either a green, orange and white jumpsuit that looked like something a crab fisherman off the coast of Alaska wears to stay dry, or they could go with a more traditional look which simply involved a pair of jeans and/or sweat pants and an untucked oversized Miami football jersey, which had to be large enough to hang to the person's knees. Up to that time, I had thought the only football fans that universally looked this stupid were from Tennessee.

Miami fans were also overly boisterous. You could hear their New Jersey by way of South Florida accents coming from two blocks away. I remember observing one Miami fan who had decided to hang out on a certain street corner and lambaste Alabama fans as they walked by. He kept yelling something about how Miami was going to kill Alabama and how Miami was so great etc., etc. For the sake of trying to decide whether this guy was just having fun or a complete moron, I decided to introduce myself. I told him that I was an Alabama fan and believed both teams clearly deserved to be in New Orleans. I also told him that I thought the two teams matched up very well and that we were in store for a good game. Not surprisingly, the man looked at me like I was crazy and proceeded to tell me in some sort of condescending fashion how Miami was going to kill Alabama.

When I asked him why he thought Miami was so much better than Alabama, he, of course, offered no factual basis or tenable reason to support his bold statement. Furthermore, when I told him that it would be interesting to see how Miami's offense could handle Alabama's defense, he simply chuckled and explained to me how Alabama was not in Miami's league. He even offered the asinine comment that, "Miami's offense could score touchdowns on the Dallas Cowboys, so he wasn't worried about no stinking Alabama defense." At this point, I realized that I was talking to a complete idiot. I couldn't help but look this guy in the face and say, "Score on the Dallas Cowboys? Yeah Right. What plant are you smoking?" Then I stated, "Oh, are you actually from Miami? I apologize for asking that question." I concluded by telling the guy that he was crazy, and then I walked away. I know it is not politically correct to stereotype an entire group of people based upon the beliefs and actions of just one person, so believe me when I say that during the three-day period I was in the Big Easy, every Miami fan I encountered reflected this same ridiculous attitude.

In addition to these delusional people, my friends and I became increasingly annoyed by the so-called football experts, such as ESPN'S Lee Corso, who continued to saturate the television in my hotel room with their so-called expert opinions about how Alabama had no chance against the Hurricanes. Had any of these clowns watched Alabama and Miami during their respective schedules that season? Miami was a team that had barely beaten an unranked Arizona team 8-7 at the Orange Bowl earlier in the season. They were also extremely fortunate to have gotten wins against both Penn State and Syracuse that year. Although those are big-name teams, neither of those teams were world beaters that season.

Furthermore, the SEC was having a banner bowl season. I believe every SEC team had won their bowl game with the exception of one going to the Sugar Bowl. Alabama's offense had already faced three defenses ranked in the top 10 in rush defense during the regular season – Louisiana Tech, Ole Miss and Auburn. Miami's rush defense was ranked somewhere in the top 10, but so what? Alabama played in the toughest conference in America. Their offense had been successful against several nationally-ranked run defenses. Miami would be no different. There was no reason to believe that Alabama would not be able to run the ball against Miami. As for Alabama's defense, Miami only scored eight points against Arizona and only 14 points against Penn State. Alabama's defense was statistically light years ahead of both of those schools. No, in my mind, the question was not whether Alabama could run the ball against Miami. Rather, the question was whether Miami could even score against

Alabama. Why couldn't these so-called experts reach this same conclusion?

After once again seeing Lee Corso rant and rave about the greatness of Miami for yet another time on the morning of the game, I decided I had had enough. I knew that ESPN was broadcasting their Sugar Bowl coverage from the mall across from the Superdome. My friend and I needed to walk down to ESPN's broadcast booth and give Corso a piece of our minds. Maybe we'd ask him to put his money where his mouth was – whatever it took. I was going to call this guy out in person, and if I was really lucky, it would take place while ESPN was on the air.

After lunch, we made our way over to the aforementioned mall. As we rode the elevator up to the second floor, I could see groups of people huddled around various broadcast tables. ESPN was set up directly in front of the elevator. It was now time to tell Mr. Corso and anybody else who would listen why Miami was not going to beat Alabama. There was just one problem. Corso was nowhere to be found. I approached a cameraman on the far side of the set and asked him where everybody was. He said that Chris Fowler, Craig James and the infamous Lee Corso were taking a broadcast break and that they would not be back for a couple of hours. A couple of hours? I didn't have time for this. The game would be starting in only three hours, and I still had to get back to my hotel room and get ready for the game.

From the corner of my eye, I saw some people huddling around another broadcast table, which was located against a sidewall to the right of ESPN's stage. I thought I heard a familiar voice talking about the football game coming from the table. As I approached, I discovered that the voice belonged to none other than long-time Birmingham sportscaster and radio personality Herb Winches. Herb was on location with his station, WJOX AM 690, out of Birmingham. Herb and his staff were allowing both Alabama and Miami fans the opportunity to offer their opinions about the upcoming game. There was a crowd of approximately 30 people surrounding the table, of which approximately half were Miami fans. The closest I could initially get to the front of the crowd was about two rows back. Not surprisingly, I heard one Miami fan after another offer their take on the game. It was just the same old "Miami is awesome…Alabama is going to get killed" crap I had been hearing the entire trip. Those comments by themselves did not bother me. Heck, by that time, I was numb to them. But when this female Miami fan decided to also proclaim "Bama sucks" – I hit the roof. I quickly darted out the left side of the crowd and made my way to the side of the broadcast table. I raised my arms, shook my hands and demanded that I be given the opportunity to respond to this woman as well as every other Miami fan in the audience who had offered their toddler-like take on the football game.

Seeing my determination to respond, Herb's colleague quickly approached me and gave me the microphone. After introducing myself to the WJOX crew and to the crowd, I proceeded to explain why Alabama would not only win the football game, but also why they very well might actually beat Miami by a large margin. I intentionally looked each and every Miami fan directly in the eye as I provided my opinion. Although it only took me only 90 seconds to provide my actual analysis of the game, I couldn't help but notice that while I was speaking, more and more Alabama fans seemed to be approaching the table. Many of the Alabama fans already in attendance were endorsing my diatribe with loud "Roll Tides," "Hell yeahs," and even a few "Amens." It was at this point I realized I had a captivated audience.

Consequently, I continued speaking.

I decided to use this opportunity to educate the Miami fans in the crowd, as well as to refresh any Alabama fans that may have forgotten, about the glory and greatness that surrounded Alabama football. From the Rose Bowls of the 1920s to the dynasties of Bear Bryant, from all of the SEC and National Championships up through the present team, which boasted the greatest defense in the history of modern day college football, everyone in attendance got a lesson in Alabama football. To my amazement, the Miami fans in the crowd slowly started to make their way to the back of the crowd. Maybe it was the eloquent yet forceful tone of my voice that had captured their attention. Maybe it was the way I emphasized each point by slamming my hand on the broadcast table. Maybe it was because I somehow found a way to use the names Copeland, Curry, Palmer and Langham in the same sentence as the Father, Son and Holy Ghost, and somehow make it make sense. I don't know. What I do know is that when I had finished my oration, most of the Miami fans in the crowd at the beginning of speech were now either long gone or were quickly departing. I concluded by leading the now fully inspired Alabama crowd with a big cheer of "Rolllllllllll Tide."

I thanked Herb Winches for the opportunity to speak, and I went on my merry way. Alabama was only two hours away from beating Miami for the national championship, and I needed to go get myself ready for the game.

When we initially arrived at the Superdome, I felt like I was at an Alabama home game. Crimson was everywhere. As we found the gate and section numbers that were on our tickets, we discovered that our seats were actually in an endzone. As we proceeded down our assigned aisle, we came to row 9. This row was the front row of the section although it actually sat 8 feet above the playing surface. A few minutes after we had reached our seats, I began to notice numerous cameras and tripods that were resting on the ground right below us. I then noticed all of the reporters, journalists and photographers that kept entering a tunnel to the right of us. I saw people wearing press badges that read Associated Press, Sporting News and even Sports Illustrated. I quickly surmised that our seats were directly in front of the press pool that was covering the game.

Once the game started, it was obvious that Alabama was more than capable of playing with Miami. Despite some missed opportunities inside the red zone, Alabama possessed a 13-6 halftime lead. During the first half, I continually noticed photographers and cameraman pointing cameras in our direction. I didn't know if they were actually taking pictures of us, but I had noticed that my friends and I had seen ourselves on the Jumbotron inside the Superdome several times.

As any Alabama fan at that game remembers, the first five minutes of the second half were absolutely magical. The play of the Alabama defense during that time span was simply phenomenal. Interceptions by both Tommy Johnson and George Teague on Miami's first two possessions sealed the game for the Crimson Tide. In every Alabama game I have ever attended before and since that wonderful night, I have never witnessed the electricity that erupted amongst Alabama fans during those five minutes. Even though there was still well over a quarter and a half of football left to be played, most Alabama fans knew that Miami was finished. (In case there were some fans still in doubt, there was a memorable play a few minutes later involving Alabama defensive back George Teague and Miami receiver Lamar Thomas that helped further usher this point home.)

I saw Chris Fowler of ESPN prowling the side lines shortly after George Teague had intercepted a Gino Torretta pass for a touchdown early in the third quarter. After several attempts,

I actually got Fowler's attention, and he approached the base of the wall on which we sat. I screamed to Fowler, "Where is Corso?" He stated something to the effect the he was back inside the stadium watching the game in a pressroom. I then asked Fowler, "What does Corso think of Miami now?" Mr. Fowler shrugged his shoulders and stated that Lee Corso was very impressed with the play of Alabama. I told Fowler that Corso should be impressed with the play of Alabama and that if Corso was any kind of man, he would offer the Alabama coaches and players a personal apology after the game for the way he wrote them off in the days and weeks before the game. Fowler nodded his head in agreement and stated that he would relay the message to his colleague. Who is to say if my comments were the impetus of what later transpired, but when we watched ESPN's post game coverage of the game, I did indeed hear the normally self-righteous, overly-pompous Mr. Corso actually make comments to that extent. Talk about playing both sides of the fence.

When the game finally ended, Alabama fans, including myself, celebrated like never before. I absolutely could not stop singing Ramma Jamma. The Alabama players had scattered across the playing field and sidelines, and every one of them was laughing and celebrating. Suddenly, I noticed an Alabama player running toward our section. He seemed to be running nearly full speed, and for a moment, I thought he might crash into the endzone wall. Right before impact, he jumped in the air and raised his arms towards us. Instinctively, my friends and I reached down and grabbed his arms. I could see by the name on the jersey that we were actually holding Alabama wide receiver Prince Wimbley. We could not stop patting him on the helmet and shoulder pads and telling him how proud we were of him and his teammates. Prince was continually screaming "Roll Tide." At one point, I thought I saw some photographers taking pictures of this celebration. After a few more seconds, Prince departed to go celebrate with the rest of his teammates. My group and I continued to celebrate inside the Superdome for several more minutes before finally departing to carry our celebration down to Bourbon Street. What a great night to be an Alabama fan.

A week after we returned to Birmingham, the media began to talk about how Sports Illustrated was coming out with a commemorative issue honoring Alabama's victory. I believe this was the first time Sports Illustrated had ever done such an issue in honor of the college football national champion. The issue came out on a Wednesday afternoon. By the time I got home that evening, my phone was ringing off the hook. One after another, various friends and family members were calling my house to inform me of my newfound fame. To my surprise, it turns out that a photographer had indeed taken a picture of my friends and me celebrating with Prince Wimbley. In fact, the photographer worked for Sports Illustrated. I know this because the picture he took became the actual back cover of the magazine.

In all, I think I bought about 30 issues. For my birthday that year, my brother gave me yet another issue. This issue, however, was signed by Alabama head coach Gene Stallings. I took this issue along with my ticket stubs of both the SEC Championship and National Championship games and had them framed together. To this day, it hangs on the wall in my study as constant reminder of our fun and glorious time in the Big Easy.

Charles D. Stewart, Jr. '02
Birmingham, Alabama

Martha Parham Hall

*"We did briefly consider lying low for a while as fugitives but we figured we wanted our parents to continue to fund our experience at our wonderful University. In the end, our better judgment prevailed, and we decided to inform the proper authorities as to our whereabouts marking the end of our student life on the run."*

*– Julie Massey*

# STUDENT LIFE
# ON THE RUN

The protocol for students at the University of Alabama was a lot different in the 60s than it is today. In those days, we had to sign in and out of our dormitories whenever we left the campus, and at night, we always had to sign out and include where we were going. We had an 11 p.m. curfew during the week and a 12 p.m. curfew on weekends. Any infraction of these rules could cause dire consequences.

My roommate and I were sort of 60s hippies (not the real thing but we did have a rebellious side), and we didn't really like to adhere to the rules. We decided that since we were older than the other students at Martha Parham dorm, we should go live in the graduate dorm. Foolishly, we thought we would have more freedom there and could do what we wanted to – when we wanted to do it. We had it all set up to move after Christmas. We even had girls moving into our old room, and they had already moved some of their stuff in before we moved out.

Before we went home for the Christmas holidays, we went to the graduate dorm to drop off some of our things. The dorm mother – yes we had those back then too – was there and said she could not wait until we moved in, and she would really watch over us like our own mothers. Wrong answer! That sounded like tighter security than we had to endure at Martha Parham, so we decided to stay at Martha Parham where there were so many students we weren't watched as closely. However, we forgot to inform the proper authorities and when we got back to school after Christmas break, we kicked out the other girls, told them to find other living quarters, and stayed in our old room. We must have been intimidating because they packed up and left with no arguments.

There was one small problem. Since we did not notify the administration or graduate dorm of our plans, we were declared missing because we were not at our registered dorm. Martha Parham was such a large dorm that The University officials hadn't located us. One of our boyfriends, who had tried to call us at the graduate dorm, finally found us and informed us of our missing persons' status. We briefly considered lying low for a while as fugitives, but we figured we wanted our parents to continue to fund our experience at our wonderful University. In the end, our better judgment prevailed and we decided to inform the proper authorities as to our whereabouts marking the end of our student life on the run.

Julie Smedley Massey '65
Knoxville, Tennessee

Photo submitted by Elise Renzetti

Snow around Denny Chimes – March 19, 1934

Brian Limbaugh and his dad, Larry Limbaugh, with victory cigars

*"My father told me that he couldn't have possibly received a better birthday present. What a way to win a basketball game. I will never forget Pettway and the buzzer beater. I was lucky enough to be there."*

*– Brian Limbaugh*

# BUZZER BEATER

It was February 23, 2002, and the men's basketball regular season was winding down. The highly ranked Florida Gators were coming to Tuscaloosa for a big SEC battle on the hardwood. It was a pivotal game for both universities and the Crimson Tide had its eye on an SEC regular season title.

I was fortunate enough to have ordered three tickets at the beginning of the season, knowing this would be a great game between the best in the East and the best in the West. It was the day before my father's, Larry Limbaugh, birthday, so I surprised him with one of those tickets. I invited another friend of mine from college, Damon McDonald, to come down and go to the game with us.

Unfortunately, the day did not begin the way we intended. We left my apartment Saturday morning from Birmingham, wanting to get to Tuscaloosa a little early to enjoy the atmosphere. We left in my Isuzu Rodeo and traveled about 15 miles before realizing I had forgotten our tickets, so we turned around and went back to my apartment to retrieve them. That was only the beginning of the frustration. We left again and were traveling down the interstate, when all of a sudden a state trooper appeared behind me and then pulled me over. Of course, the very gracious trooper gave me a ticket for speeding in a construction zone – a double fine. Obviously, there was not any construction going on at the time, and as usual, other cars were passing me, but I was the one singled out and ticketed. This made for a memorable start.

We finally arrived in Tuscaloosa and entered Coleman Coliseum to a sold out crowd, hopefully there to watch the Tide pull off a big upset over the Gators. The pre-game announcement of the starting lineups was truly electric. The lights went off, highlights of the Tide on the big screen, and the Bama faithful were going wild. It was now time to tip it off and get it on.

It was a back and forth game as the lead swapped many times. Florida would get ahead, but Bama would quickly come back as the game went down to the wire. Florida was up by one point with only seconds left on the clock. My heart was already pounding with excitement and nervousness from all the intensity as I thought to myself, "Can we really beat them or is this going to be another heartbreak?" At that very moment, the Tide took the ball down the court and almost turned it over, but freshman Earnest Shelton saved the ball, passed it to an open Antoine Pettway, who laid it in at the buzzer.

Bama wins! Bama wins!

The crowd went crazy! The students rushed onto the court. It was total mayhem. We danced in the aisles, pinching ourselves to make sure what we saw had really taken place. I looked up at the scoreboard and saw: Bama 65. . . Florida 64. The fans began to chant, "SEC, SEC," as everyone realized that Alabama had just clinched the SEC regular season title.

That was the most exciting basketball game that I have ever seen in person. It was a great culmination to a day that began with real frustration. My father told me that he couldn't have possibly received a better birthday present. What a way to win a basketball game. I will never forget Pettway and the buzzer beater. I was lucky enough to be there!

Brian Limbaugh
Birmingham, Alabama

Brian and Keisha Limbaugh, moments after
finding out their baby will be a little girl.

Ingrid Probst (daughter), Brenda Ford, Cynthia Raulston (daughter) and Stacy Probst (daughter)

*"Men are absolutely amazing when it comes to football total recall. Even though they can't remember birthdays, anniversaries or even how old their kids are, they somehow have a photographic memory of the exact time remaining on the clock when the game-deciding play occurred."*

*– Brenda Ford*

# LET'S PUT IT
# IN PERSPECTIVE

When I think back to my days at the University in the 60s… remembering "the way things were" in the "good ol' days" of Bama football, I cannot remember a specific game, particular quarter or which down a brilliant play was executed. Even though my future husband (in a former life) played football for Bear Bryant while I was in school, my memories were often quite different. In many ways times have changed, but in other ways, they are exactly the same.

Men… are absolutely amazing when it comes to football total recall. Even though they can't remember birthdays, anniversaries or even how old their kids are, they somehow have a photographic memory of the exact time remaining on the clock when the game-deciding play occurred.

Women… remember the important Cliff Notes versions, who won the Iron Bowl that year, or whether Alabama was National Champion.

Men… remember starting offensive linemen, team defense rankings and what automatic bowl bids are tied to the top six teams in the SEC.

Women… remember the yearly vacation that comes with a bowl game and pray for a sunny beach or snow capped mountains rather than a trip to lovely Shreveport, Louisiana.

Men… remember and agonize over the bad or lucky calls, and sometimes the name of the referee who made the call. They will even tune into sports talk radio for hours as callers argue whether his foot was "in" or "out."

Women… remember if their dyed-to-match outfit worn to the game was a success, who they saw at the game and who wore cute shoes.

Men… remember what buddy came over to watch the game and boldly picked a 17-point underdog to win while everyone told him he was crazy.

Women… remember the great cheese ball their girlfriend brought over and how excited she was to get the recipe.

Men… remember extremely cold, wet games and wear as a badge of courage the fact that, due to superstition, they refused to put on their poncho on the final drive so they are now home from work on a Monday in bed with no voice and a 103-degree fever.

Women… remember thinking how stupid the guys were, standing out in the rain to see the game when Bama was up by 21, while they went under the stands, sipped hot chocolate and watched the game on closed circuit television.

If you're a man and reading this, you are probably thinking… what do women know? And who cares what shoes I wear to the game? And women you are thinking… who cares that John Doe is fifth on the middle linebacker depth chart?

The bottom line is that times may change, but some things will always remain the same!

Brenda Ford '68
Birmingham, Alabama

# BRUSH WITH GREATNESS

I'm not an Alabama fan, but one thing happened to me in Tuscaloosa a few years ago, which I want to share with all Bama fans.

I was visiting some friends in Tuscaloosa for a Saturday game, and we were all tailgating. Then, in front of me, not more than 20 yards away, walked a well known Bama legend. Well, you don't really have to be an Alabama fan to recognize or admire someone with these credentials, so I called out his name and asked him to come over and meet all my friends. Smiling, he did so, and shook hands with each and every one of them.

As he began to leave, I asked him if he would mind signing the program that I had purchased. Being a huge college football fan, I thought it would be a great autograph to have. As he turned and looked at me, he said with the most serious look he could give, "Well, that depends... you got a beer for me?" He smiled! I quickly gave him a beer, he signed my program and I thanked him for the autograph. He hung around for a few more minutes, thanked me for the beer, and off he went.

The thing that I remember most was here is one of the greatest college football players of all time, and he treated me and everyone else just like normal people... and he even had a beer with us!

Joey Campbell
Montgomery, Alabama

Heidi and Somerville Evans
Sao Paulo, Brazil

*"Here in Brazil the seasons are opposite of those in the northern hemisphere, and on chilly, wintry July days, when there is a crisp quality to the air, my husband and I are sure to give each other a quick glance and simultaneously utter, 'It feels like tailgating weather!'"*

*– Heidi Evans*

— 𝒜 —

# ALABAMA FUTEBOL

A s a 1999 alumnus of the University of Alabama School of Law, it's hard enough being married to an Auburn fan, but try following your beloved Crimson Tide from the other side of the equator, 5,000 miles away from home.

In 2002, my job as a foreign diplomat with the State Department took me (and the aforementioned Auburn fan husband) to the Consulate General of the United States in Sao Paulo, Brazil, where we have lived and worked for the last 18 months. Moving to Brazil, we essentially traded "football" for "futebol," as soccer is known in Portuguese, and despite the ardor for local professional sports teams such as the Sao Paulo Futebol Clube, the Corinthians and Pele's old team, Santos, to me nothing can replace the excitement of feeling the metal I-beams of Bryant-Denny Stadium shake as the elephant roar blares over the sound system heralding the beginning of a game, or hearing the slow, opening chords of "Yea, Alabama!" played by the Million Dollar Band, knowing the revelry and fanfare that are sure to come next.

Here in Brazil the seasons are opposite of those in the northern hemisphere, and on chilly, wintry July days, when there is a crisp quality to the air, my husband and I are sure to give each other a quick glance and simultaneously utter, "It feels like tailgating weather!" And if we get too sentimental, we can watch one of the many Alabama and Auburn football games our parents have recorded off of TV and sent to us in the mail, which tends to arrive two or three weeks after the actual game has taken place (we do have cable TV, but ESPN International only shows such important sporting events as the World Cricket Finals or beach volleyball, and then usually covered by Spanish-speaking commentators). The only other option for "watching games" is to stay glued for hours at a time to our home computer, watching internet-based virtual game simulcasts on ESPN or CBS Sportsline's websites. But even then, the time-zone difference works against us, with games taking place either two, three or four hours ahead of Central Time, depending on what time of the year it is in Brazil (the time difference changes with the seasonal changes). I must admit, I have stayed up until 3 a.m. "watching" such games on more than one occasion.

Despite the foregoing, I am still a Crimson Tide faithful, keeping up with the scores as best as I can. Lack of TV access alone is not enough to keep me from following my favorite team, all the way from Brazil, and it certainly will not be enough to keep me from following the Crimson Tide next year, when my husband and I move to the other side of the International Date Line for our next assignment.

Heidi Bartlett Evans '99.
Sao Paulo, Brazil

Somerville and Heidi Evans
Parati, Brazil

Summer and Joe Basgier

*"Six months later, Joe proposed at the lighting of the White House Christmas tree in Washington D.C., and we were married on August 30, 2003. Those same friends and colleagues from law school have pulled us back to the South, so that we may now call Alabama our home."*

*– Summer Basgier*

# THE TIDE THAT BINDS

As a little girl in Birmingham, Alabama, I was always surrounded by a family of avid Alabama fans. I remember watching Alabama football games very early in life, and one of my earliest Alabama memories is watching Bear Bryant's funeral on television when I was four years old. As the years passed, I attended Legion Field games and watched other games on television with my parents. I became a true Alabama fan while watching the Tide win the National Championship in 1992, my freshman year in high school.

After graduation, there was never any doubt I would attend the University of Alabama, and in the fall of 1995 I moved to Tuscaloosa for my freshman year. I immediately fell in love with Tuscaloosa, so much that my four years at Alabama seemed to somehow fly by. Before long, I had decided to stay three more years and attend the University of Alabama School of Law in 1999. Little did I know I would be forever bound to The University.

Meanwhile, a guy named Joe was growing up in Virginia Beach, Virginia, as a huge Redskins fan. Because of this, he didn't pay much attention to college football, not to mention Crimson Tide football. Joe attended James Madison University in Virginia, and by some twist of fate, he also decided to enroll in Alabama Law School in 1999.

Through mutual friends in law school, Joe and I were always at the same parties and had classes together. But it wasn't until our third year of law school that we started to become good friends. After two years in Tuscaloosa, Joe had become a huge Alabama fan, and he had developed just the slightest southern drawl. We started talking often and coordinating dinner with friends or a night out on the town.

We spent the fall of 2001 going to football games, planning tailgating parties and thoroughly enjoying our last football season in Tuscaloosa. When we came back for spring semester, Joe and I grew even closer, going to class during the day, having lunch at Mike and Ed's BBQ or Crimson Café, spending the afternoon at the cliffs, by the pool and planning dinner parties at my condo at Capstone Condominiums or on Joe's front porch on 13th Street. Sometimes we'd get a group of friends together to go to local watering holes, like Jackie's, Innisfree or the Venue.

By spring break of that semester, Joe and I were talking every day and spending most afternoons together studying, enjoying Tuscaloosa, or hanging out with our group of friends at night. When people would ask if we were dating, we both denied that we were anything more than friends, but soon that would all change.

Joe and I started dating two days before law school graduation. He called me that morning, and we picked up lunch from Crimson Café, took it to the quad and ate while sitting on the steps of Denny Chimes. Then we walked around campus taking pictures of the president's mansion, the Quad, Foster Auditorium, Bryant-Denny Stadium and the Ferguson Center. That night, our group of friends had dinner at Kirkwood Mansion, an antebellum home located in Eutaw, Alabama. Joe and I came back to Tuscaloosa that night, and while sitting and talking on Joe's front porch, we realized we were more than just friends.

We were excited that we had both made plans to move to Washington, D.C., after law school, and we started making plans to live in the same neighborhood. Leaving Tuscaloosa was hard, but we felt like we were taking a little piece of The University with us. We made the big move and slowly settled into city life. New jobs to adjust to and a new city to explore kept us busy, but along the way we grew even closer. That fall we made time to return to the Capstone for Homecoming to reminisce and cheer on the Tide.

Six months later, Joe proposed at the lighting of the White House Christmas tree in Washington D.C., and we were married on August 30, 2003. Those same friends and colleagues from law school have pulled us back to the South, so that we now call Alabama our home. In the fall of 2003, we traveled to "T-town" to tailgate, eat and drink with family and good friends, and remember the place where it all began.

Summer Drummonds Basgier '98 & '02
Birmingham, Alabama

Paul Lawson at Sewell-Thomas Stadium

*"Frick–a name that through the years has been
synonymous with baseball. This particular Frick
was an Alabama catcher named Matt. He stood
at home plate at Sewell-Thomas Stadium in the
bottom of the 10th with two out and a 3-2 count.
Alabama and mighty Southern California
were tied 8-8."*

*– Paul Lawson*

# NO SADNESS IN MUDVILLE ON THIS BAMA DAY

Alabama 9 – Southern California 8

Frick – a name that through the years has been synonymous with baseball. This particular Frick was an Alabama catcher named Matt. He stood at home plate at Sewell-Thomas Stadium in the bottom of the 10th with two out and a 3-2 count. Alabama and mighty Southern California were tied 8-8.

Following Alabama baseball in the 1970s was easy. I would pick up the next day's newspaper and check the scores to see if the Tide had won. Games were not on the radio, at least outside of Tuscaloosa, and they were played in front of mostly parents and close friends, without much hoopla. But the 1980s and 1990s would change it all and put Bama baseball on the map.

Even in the 70s, there were a few highlights. Butch Hobson helped lead the Tide to a division title in the early 70s and then went on to play for the Boston Red Sox. Former major league stars, Pee-Wee Reese and Elston Howard, sent their sons to wear the crimson and white. George Steinbrenner brought the New York Yankees to town as a favor for Coach Paul "Bear" Bryant.

Then came 1983. Alabama won as never before with a school record of 46 wins, a sweep through the SEC tournament in

Starkville and the NCAA Regional in Tallahassee, Florida. All of a sudden, Bama baseball was on the map and playing in the College World Series in Omaha. I was delighted to see my alma mater playing Arizona State with Barry Bonds, beating Michigan and its stars Barry Larkin and Chris Sabo, as well as Texas with its ace, Roger Clemens. ESPN was showing the Tide play baseball. We finished number two in the nation in 1983. I couldn't wait for next year.

But next year became 12 years more, and Bama baseball was both good and bad, but never again Omaha bound. Then Coach Jim Wells arrived, and Alabama baseball started to climb back into the national spotlight. The first year, in 1995, there was a NCAA Regional final and, in 1996, another rung in the ladder with a school record 50 wins and a trip to Omaha. Then came 1997. Something truly great was about to happen.

It was Sunday, May 25, 1997, and NCAA Regional Finals time in Tuscaloosa, Alabama. The Tide had beaten Troy State, Wichita State and North Carolina State and faced the tradition-rich Trojans of Southern California, winners of 11 baseball national championships. My brother and I arrived at the ballpark a good two hours before game time. We couldn't have known the drama that was about to unfold. It began with disheartening news. The Tide's Roberto Vaz, one of the top five players in America, had stepped on a baseball after batting practice and had broken his foot.

The game was filled with tension from the start. Each team held the lead. Back and forth the momentum swung as one hoped to put away the other. Late in the game, the Trojans' All-American Eric Munson was on second base with two outs. With the game tied, a base hit would surely put the Trojans ahead. Southern Cal got the hit they needed—a single to left. But the Crimson Tide had the left fielder we needed – All-American G.W. Keller. He fielded and gunned a throw to home, nailing the Trojan star for the third out. It was just enough to send the game into extra innings. Alabama stopped a rally in the ninth inning with a double play. Southern Cal turned back the Tide with a double play of its own. In the top of the tenth, Alabama responded with yet another twin-killing.

I know my blood pressure was off the scale as the game moved to the bottom of the tenth. Bama made two quick outs and it looked like the game would move to yet another extra inning. Then it happened. Matt Frick, Bama's catcher, came to bat, and Hollywood itself could not have written a better script. The count was three balls two strikes, and Frick belted a tremendous home run over the left centerfield fence. Ballgame over – Alabama 9 - Southern California 8.

I will never forget the yell of the crowd and the UA radio broadcast at that moment. Bama's Sports Information Director for Baseball, Barry Allen, was calling the game. As Matt Frick circled the bases, Allen screamed to all of those tuned in, "We are going to Omaha!!"

It was a moment for all who love the Crimson and White to cherish. "We live and die by the home run," Alabama Coach Jim Wells said. "Frick's might have been the biggest ever."

Indeed it was, Coach. Indeed it was. I will never forget it.

Paul Lawson '75
Birmingham, Alabama

Mary Hill's husband, Danny, and Big Al

*"What seemed to start out as a dreadful day
became one of our best tailgating trips ever.
We probably check a little closer now as we
pack for our trips to T-town, but rest assured,
knowing there are always Bama fans around
to help a friend in need."*

*– Mary Hill*

# TAILGATING HOSPITALITY

Tailgating is one of my favorite pastimes and what better occasion than the first game of the season in Tuscaloosa against Oklahoma on September 6, 2003?

We left Birmingham bright and early to get our usual spot. As we loaded the car, we ran though the checklist... flags... shakers... signs... tickets... The excitement grew as we passed fellow Tide fans the closer we got to T-town.

We pulled in and found our new spot for the year then began to set up the tent, inflate Big Al, and unload the food, but that's when we realized we only had our small cooler, so the only food we packed was the hamburger meat.

Wonderful, our well-planned tailgating experience was ruined! As we discussed what to do, one of the nearby tailgaters, whom we had never met before, realized what happened and offered us some of their food. From there, word spread and before we knew it, fans all around chipped in until we had more than we could eat in two days.

What seemed to start out as a dreadful day became one of our best tailgating trips ever. We probably check a little closer now as we pack for our trips to T-town, but rest assured, there are always Bama fans around to help a friend in need.

Mary Hill
Birmingham, Alabama

Shanna Moore's Birthday
Shanna Moore and Lex Tiffin
Auburn, Alabama – December 2, 1989

*"Our best holiday of the year for our family was by far, Thanksgiving, and not so much that we especially loved Thanksgiving, but that it was usually the weekend of two great things… our daughter's birthday celebration and the Iron Bowl. From 1984 through 1998 I can count on one hand the number of Bama games that we did not attend in our RV and some of our best memories of friends and family come from these times."*

*– Kelly Moore*

# ON THE ROAD AGAIN

Our family has spent most of our lives centered around one great family tradition. It's not Christmas, Easter, or the 4th of July, even though we celebrate those with each other. Our best holiday of the year for our family was by far, Thanksgiving, and not so much that we especially loved Thanksgiving, but it was usually the weekend of two great things… our daughter's birthday celebration and the Iron Bowl. From 1984 through 1998, I can count on one hand the number of Bama games that we did not attend in our RV, and some of our best memories of friends and family come from these times.

In 1984, there were not a lot of RVs at Bama games. We were a very close group of fans that spent two to four days before games perfecting grilling techniques, sharing stories, and warming up opposing fans to the Bama Nation that would soon descend on their campus and destroy their football team… with class, of course.

In these early days of RVing, I suddenly became a celebrity within our small group of fans. It was 6 a.m., and I heard a knock on our door. Surely, this was not someone knocking on my door at 6 a.m. on the morning of the game, but sure enough, I opened the door and there was a fellow RVer who proceeded to explain that the electricity and generator on his RV was not working and he had 40 people coming over for lunch that day. We ventured over to his RV and found that one of the switches in the electrical box had gone bad. Luckily, I had learned a trick of putting a penny between the switch as a temporary fix, and the RV was up and running in no time. Later that day we were showered with more food and random people thanking us than we could imagine, and it was then that I became dubbed the RV mechanic.

Over the years, we had our chance of being on TV as well. There were two times in particular that I remember. One was when we were at Legion Field for the Alabama vs. Notre Dame game. Keith Jackson decided he would broadcast from what he described as the RV Nation and stood next to our RV as he delivered his pre-game show. We got the opportunity to talk with him before the broadcast, and he described his passion for being at Bama games and spending time with fans that truly understand the game of football. The other was when my good friend and tailgater, Skipper Falls, from Tuscaloosa, was grilling Cornish hens before the Iron Bowl. The local news team made their way around to our tailgating site and asked us what we were grilling. Skipper just smiled and opened the lid of the grill. I picked up one of the Cornish hens with a grilling fork and held it to the camera. Skipper smiled into the camera and simply said, "Baby eagles of course!" We beat Auburn that game and our grilling footage was all over the local news.

Back in the "early days" of tailgating, we traveled to Penn State on a couple of occasions, and I can truly say the Penn State fans are the classiest and most gracious fans in the world. Our first trip to Penn State in 1986 yielded a very prominent Bama fan that proceeded to park his RV right on main street. For all of game day he blasted "Yea Alabama" over the loud speaker, and in between, he would get on the microphone and announce – "Weather Alert! Weather Alert! The National Weather Service has placed State College under a high Tide warning for later today." Unfortunately, we did not win the game that day, but afterwards, the avid Tide fan got back on his loud speaker and took his medicine.

"Attention, an update from the weather service… the earlier forecast for the Tide warning did not materialize as expected." That game ended in controversy as a Tide receiver clearly caught a pass in the end zone to win the game but was called out of bounds. Later that night, we heard a knock on our RV door. I opened the door and a Penn State fan stood there. He proceeded to apologize for the call in the end zone and stated that we should have won the game. Did I mention that the State fans are extremely classy?

Another great trip to Happy Valley is when I got a call from my good friend, Bob Tiffin. It was Thursday and he asked if I wanted to drive up to the Bama vs. Penn State game. I told him it was a little late to be making plans to drive to the game, but he went on to explain that the game had not been scheduled to be on TV and therefore the cheerleaders were not going to make the trip. At the last minute, ABC decided to carry the game and the cheerleaders needed a way to the ballgame. We left Thursday afternoon and drove all night to get the cheerleaders to Happy Valley on Friday. On the drive up, Bob was driving the RV in front of me and he was pulling his blazer behind him. The cheerleaders had stuck the Big Al suit in the back of the Blazer with the head facing out the back window. I can't begin to tell you how many cars would start to pass my RV, see the Big Al head in the back of the Blazer on the RV in front of me, and then slow down to confirm what they had just seen. I guess Big Al gets attention everywhere he goes.

Speaking of opposing fans, Penn State may have the classiest fans, but Ohio State has the most trash-talking. We went to the 1977 Sugar Bowl, and for some reason, we ended up staying at the Marriott, which housed 90 percent of the Ohio State contingent that week. Every time I left my room, the Ohio State fans would heckle me. There was one fan in particular that seemed to be in the lobby or on the elevator every time I left the hotel, and he would proceed to tell me "how bad the Buckeyes were going to beat Bama" and "he didn't understand why I even bothered to come to New Orleans." At the end of the week, I finally asked the obnoxious fan for his room number so I could call him after the game and discuss the result. He gladly gave it to me. As we all know, Bama won that game, and I could not wait to get back to the hotel and call my new Buckeye friend. He answered the phone and immediately starting laughing when he heard my voice. He reluctantly stated that Bama was by far the better team and he was going to be eating his words for breakfast in the morning.

Of all the great memories I have from tailgating over the years, my favorite times were during Iron Bowl week. From Wednesday through Sunday, we would get together with the RV nation and cook elaborate Thanksgiving meals and share stories about previous Iron Bowls. We would also take a cake with us that week and celebrate our daughter's birthday. If you have never spent three days parked outside of Legion Field surrounded by Alabama and Auburn fans, I can only say that you are missing out. The excitement and build-up of being in that atmosphere for so long is incredible and by the time kick off comes, you are boiling with intensity. It is a feeling I will never forget and often times miss when the season ends. Over the last few years, we haven't been able to make it to as many games as we used to, but I will never forget the wonderful friends we made and how many great memories have come along with hitting the road again to see the Tide play on Saturday.

Kelly Moore
Red Bay, Alabama

Philden Stockton, Greta Stockton, Kreg Kennedy, Kurt Kennedy,
Brandon (Shanna and Kelly Moore in background) after game in '92

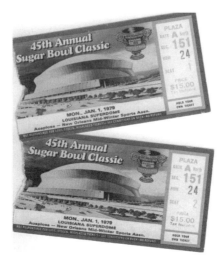

Linda and Terry Birchfield's
ticket stubs from the 1979 Sugar Bowl

*"It was 1979 and I had been married for 10 years
to my wonderful husband, Terry. That was when I
received one of the best anniversary presents ever.
Some women may think of jewelry, romantic
dinners or a sweet letter or poem, but my
husband nailed it with a pair of tickets to the
45th Annual Sugar Bowl Classic."*

*– Linda Birchfield*

# THE GOAL-LINE ANNIVERSARY

I have been an Alabama fan for as long as I can remember. Everybody knows in this state, it's one or the other. You're either Alabama or Auburn. With all the tradition surrounding the Alabama program, I don't see how anyone could not choose Alabama. My choice was made long ago, and I am a tried and true Bama fan.

There is one memory that holds a very special place in my heart. It was 1979, and I had been married for 10 years to my wonderful husband, Terry. That was when I received one of the best anniversary presents ever. Some women may think of jewelry, romantic dinners, or a sweet letter or poem, but my husband nailed it with a pair of tickets to the 45th Annual Sugar Bowl Classic. I was so excited. Football does crazy things to women down here.

We headed to New Orleans, and before we knew it, we were standing even with the now famous goal line in the corner of the dome. Tony Nathan's parents were seated a few rows down from us which we thought was really cool. It was a game for the ages as the Tide rose up in the end with a truly inspiring stand to salvage what surely looked like the end. Seeing Bear up close was awesome. I will never forget that day as long as I live.

About six years ago, my son-in-law, Mark, and my daughter, Ginger, gave me the picture of the Goal Line Stand as a birthday present because Mark had heard me say that of all the Championship prints, I would want that one the most. It is now prominently displayed in our home.

Over the many wonderful years that my family has followed the Tide, I know Alabama will always be great because of the tradition and spirit that is instilled in every team – teams that give all they have every time they step on the field. It is that exact reason why Bama is and will always be in a class by itself.

ROLL TIDE ROLL!

Linda Birchfield
Hope Hull, Alabama

Terry Birchfield, Gene Stallings and Linda Birchfield

Vicki Massler Middlebrooks with the winning ticket

*"When I looked up, there was Coach Bryant.
He was looking straight down at me as he
said in that low, slow southern drawl…
"Suck it up and go, Dahlin'."
He walked off and I just stood there. It is
amazing how a brief moment can teach you a
lesson you remember for the rest of your life."*

*– Vicki Middlebrooks*

# THE WINNING TICKET

I n the late spring semester of my junior year in 1971, I was worried and very concerned about getting enough money to go to summer school so I could take some extra courses in order to graduate in May 1972. It was raining and I had had a lot of tests and papers due. I was stressed to the max. I was walking in the pouring rain from the library across the quad with my head down, soaking wet and crying. Suddenly, I ran into a man. When I looked up, there was Coach Bryant. He was looking straight down at me as he said in that low, slow southern drawl… "Suck it up and go, Dahlin." He walked off, and I just stood there. It is amazing how a brief moment can teach you a lesson you remember for the rest of your life.

Years later, during graduate school, I worked at Greene Track in Eutaw, Alabama. I was working in the club house as a cashier. Coach Bryant and Mrs. Mary Harmon often frequented the track on Saturday nights. Soon, Coach Bryant was coming to my window on a regular basis to cash his tickets. I would get so nervous. He would cash his ticket and then wink at me as he walked off. One night I told myself that if he came to my window, I was going to ask for his autograph. Finally, I did it and he signed the back of his winning ticket "Paul W. Bryant." I had to get permission from my supervisor to keep the ticket, and he politely agreed due to the unique circumstances. Through all these years, I have always known where that ticket was and when they came out with the special edition "Paul 'Bear' Bryant" stamps… I got a sheet of them in a nice crisp sleeve that had his profile in the "hat". I had the autographed winning ticket and the stamps framed which now hangs in our den.

I'm not sure if Coach Bryant's wink at my ticket window was to acknowledge he remembered our first encounter, but every time I see "The Winning Ticket," I'm reminded to just "Suck it up and go, Dahlin'!"

Vicki Massler Middlebrooks '72 & '76
Herndon, Virginia

# A BAMA BIRTHDAY

While in high school, back in Ozark, Alabama, I was good friends with Dexter Wood who was good friends with John Croyle. For my 21st birthday, my mama called Dexter to ask him to buy my birthday cake and bring it to my dorm room at Mary Burke West as a surprise. At that time, I was "mad" about Johnny Musso (that means I really liked him for you young folks). That afternoon, Dexter and John came to the dorm, unannounced, and brought me a huge cake along with a huge autographed poster of the "Italian Stallion." I guess you could say that was one of the best birthdays I ever had!

Vicki Massler Middlebrooks '72 & '76
Herndon, Virginia

Britt Thames, Al Blanton and Jordan Baird

*My mother has had the privilege of living with Big Al for 34 years. Unfortunately for her, I'm not talking about the big red elephant that makes children smile every Saturday in the fall. This is another animal known as my father, Big Al Blanton.*

*– Al Davis Blanton*

# BIG AL AND THE BARBEQUE GALS

My mother has had the privilege of living with Big Al for 34 years. Unfortunately for her, I'm not talking about the big red elephant that makes children smile every Saturday in the fall. This is another animal known as my father, Big Al Blanton. Luckily for me, my dad's impatience would eventually produce one of the greatest memories of my childhood.

My dad is a character in the purest sense of the word. He stands about six feet two inches tall and tips the scales at a "feathery" 260 pounds. He's as stubborn as a bull, will fight at the drop of a hat, and has the loudest mouth this side of the Mississippi.

He can usually be seen at local coffee shops and other establishments sipping a large coffee and taking multiple tugs on a fresh pack of Kool cigarettes. But what makes this man distinct is his genuine love for me and my mother.

I will always be thankful for all the times my dad took me to Alabama football games when I was a child. Because of him, I grew up loving the Tide. We would go to all of the Legion Field games, park in the same spot, then leave the game early to beat the post-game traffic.

Due to the fact that my father and I had developed a system of traveling to and from the games, we always had an opportunity to notice all of the sights and sounds along Eighth Avenue in front of Legion Field. Typically, there were numerous vendors offering a wide assortment of Tide memorabilia and others trying to make a buck off the day's events.

As we neared the stadium, I would always look forward to the smell of barbeque in the air, as well as the gracious ladies that had prepared it. We would often stop for a barbeque sandwich or a hamburger and catch the scores on a small black-and-white television that was nearby.

On the third Saturday in October 1993, my father and I traveled in usual fashion to the Alabama-Tennessee game. We found our usual spot, walked down Eighth Avenue, stopped for a barbeque, then headed to the game. I was particularly nervous about this game because Alabama had not lost to Tennessee in seven years and had not lost at all in nearly two seasons.

We found our spot inside Legion Field and watched a dismal Tide offense produce only 9 points through three-and-a-half quarters. I wanted to stay for the duration of the game, but then came those inevitable words from my father. We walked through the gates of Legion Field, and I was certain we had lost. My dad put his arm around me to give me comfort, but I was still upset. As we were making our way back to the car, I noticed that a group of people were cheering and gathering around that old black-and-white TV set near the barbeque joint.

Just as I was running over to find out what all the commotion was about, someone yelled, "We're driving!" When I glanced at the set, I saw Jay Barker at Alabama's 40-yard-line. Although we hadn't moved the ball much in the second half,

I knew that Barker would lead us down the field. With each pass that Barker completed, a larger and larger crowd began to gather around the old TV set, and the smiles on the faces of the cooks got bigger and bigger.

The crowd eventually got so big that people were jumping up to catch a glimpse of the game. I can still see those fans jockeying for position in front of the set. The Tide finally scored to make it 17-15, and it was pandemonium. The noise eventually settled as we waited for the two-point conversion. As Bama took to the huddle, a guy near the front said, "Palmer's in at quarterback!" As David Palmer received the ball and took it around right end, the crowd went crazy. I happened to see his feet cross the plain of the endzone, and all I could do was jump in the air. Everyone around me was hugging, crying, and giving each other multiple high-fives.

I know in my heart that if the game had gone to overtime, we would have beaten Tennessee. But I was proud of the fact that the Tide had enough courage to produce one final drive behind Jay Barker and David Palmer.

On the way back to the car, I thanked my dad for taking me to the game. In true Big Al fashion, he said, "See, I knew we should have left the game early." We shared a laugh, then made our way back to our house. My mom was there, waiting with a smile and a big "Roll Tide."

Al Davis Blanton '02
Birmingham, Alabama

# WATCHING MY COUSIN IN IRON BOWL 1971

I was 10 years old when I attended my first Iron Bowl. Since my cousin, Johnny Musso, was a star running back for the Crimson Tide at that time, it came as no surprise that I wore a replica #22 Alabama jersey for the occasion. It was a game I would never forget.

The term "the tension in the air was so thick, you could cut it with a knife" has never been more appropriate than it was on this particular afternoon at Legion Field. The stakes were high. Both teams were undefeated and, put simply, whoever won was going to the Orange Bowl to play Nebraska for the national championship. It was a familiar setting for the Tide, but far from ordinary for Auburn.

As luck would have it, our seats were right next to a group of obnoxious Auburn fans. One man was so confident that Auburn would prevail, he tried to bet my mother $100 that her beloved Tide would fall. For whatever reason, my father just ignored the guy, but I was more than perturbed that a total stranger would try to wager with my mom. Much to my delight, an Alabama fan finally took the bet, a decision the Auburn boaster would soon live to regret.

During the week leading up to the game, there was a lot of controversy which fueled the bad blood between opposing fans. Auburn quarterback Pat Sullivan had just won the

Heisman Trophy, but the Bama nation strongly felt that Johnny Musso rightfully deserved the award. Had the Heisman voting taken place one week later, I cannot help but think that Musso would have easily won the trophy.

Musso came into the 1971 Iron Bowl hampered by a broken toe, and seeing him in pre-game warm-ups convinced me that he probably would not play. I could not have been more wrong. Not only did Musso play, but he amazingly rushed for 167 yards and scored two touchdowns. On the other hand, the Heisman trophy winner's day was not as productive, as Auburn's Sullivan faced a vicious pass rush the entire game, disrupting his rhythm and usually leaving him flat on his back.

Alabama won that game 31-7, but the score should have been much worse. Alabama fans were ecstatic, and Auburn fans were stunned, none more so than the jerk who had to part with his $100. I can remember it like it happened yesterday rather than more than three decades ago. Being able to see my cousin run up and down the field while I proudly sported that replica #22 jersey in the midst of hostile AU fans made the 1971 Iron Bowl one I will never forget.

David Murray
Birmingham, Alabama

Kristi and Holli Lawson with Big Al, 1984

*"The next morning, we all awoke at the same time to a strange noise outside. My mother jumped from the bed to look out the window and exclaimed, 'We have entered the twilight zone!' My father asked what she was talking about. She continued, 'I think that we're in Auburn.'"*

*— Kristi Lawson*

# A LAWSON FAMILY ROADTRIP

As a child growing up in Hoover, Alabama, there were two constants in my young life – church on the first day of the week and a University of Alabama sporting event on the last. Throughout these impressionable years, I have many wonderful memories of Alabama football, baseball and basketball. Of all the great Alabama moments I shared with my family, a trip to the Bluegrass state in the fall of 1988 is one of the most memorable.

My father, Paul, announced two weeks before the match-up with Kentucky that the Lawson family would journey to Lexington to see the mighty Alabama football team take on the Wildcats of Kentucky. Dad is among the most intense Tide fans that one will encounter and a great historian of the storied tradition of the University of Alabama. To prepare us for the game, he prepared our game film of Kentucky. That's right, he has a complete library of every televised Alabama game dating back to the invention of the VCR. After we reviewed the film, my father would end our studies with a refresher course of the team rosters.

Prior to departure, my dad was responsible for gathering the Tide gear, and he made sure to pack all flags, shakers, cushion seats, and any other vital gear that displayed the name of the Crimson Tide. If these items didn't display an officially licensed emblem of the University of Alabama, they wouldn't go.

My mother, Connie was responsible for all other away game preparations. Several days in advance of our departure, she started cooking. The sweet smell of cookies, brownies and many other delicious snacks filled the kitchen. She prepared food, drinks, clothing and anything else her family would possibly need for the two-day journey. We have never quite understood how she could prepare so much by herself. We often wondered if 15 other people would be joining us on the trip because there was no way our family could eat all that food.

With my father and mother's preparations complete, my sister Holli and I loaded into the car for the long drive to Lexington. We knew that we were in for a long drive, but my dad had prepared for this as well. As we drove, we listened to sports talk analysis, taped replays of great Alabama moments, and in between we listened to dad's pontification of the team, the coach and of the game to come. All the while, we stuffed ourselves with the tasty treats my mom had prepared. As the sugar high began to wear off, my sister and I faded off into a good nap.

We awoke to the sound of a debate between my parents. It was dark now, and the subject of the debate was a particular road and whether or not we should turn around. I'm not sure who won this debate, but the sign "Welcome to Ohio" quickly told us that we had gone the wrong way. After some deliberation, we decided to find the closest hotel and regroup the next morning. My parents were getting tired and didn't seem to know exactly where we were, but the bright lights of a hotel were a welcome sign to us all.

The next morning, we all awoke at the same time to a strange noise outside. My mother jumped from the bed to look out the window and exclaimed, "We have entered the twilight zone!" My father asked what she was talking about. She continued, "I think that we're in Auburn." With that, we all ran to the window to see for ourselves. My father began laughing uncontrollably as we looked at three large cows directly under our window. At the late hour of the previous night, no one had bothered to look out the rear window of our room. If we had, we might have seen the giant field with hundreds of cows meandering around, reminiscent to a scene you might find down on the plains of Auburn. After the laughter subsided, my parents studied the map and we loaded up for the remaining trip into Lexington.

We arrived in Lexington with time to spare. We drove around town so that my dad could find a good spot for lunch. Actually, the rest of the family knew that he was simply looking for Burger King. Why Burger King, you may ask? The answer is simple – Alabama was something like 8 and 0 when the Lawson family ate our pre-game meal at Burger King. This was one of dad's many game day superstitions, but there are probably not enough pages in this book to go further into this subject. This was acceptable, however, as Holli and I had developed a fondness for the Jr. Whopper.

We finally reached game time, the sole purpose for this long road trip. We filed into our seats to watch another Tide victory. The sky looked a bit ominous and looked like rain. It was then we learned my dad had made a critical flaw in packing our gear. He had forgotten our Alabama ponchos. As the rain began, I volunteered to go with my dad to search for gear to keep our family dry throughout the day. We traveled throughout the stadium from booth to booth, but not one single vendor had an Alabama poncho. We had only found Kentucky ponchos, and they were selling out quickly. I remember watching my father face this moral dilemma and I could just imagine him weighing the options between wearing the propaganda of his enemy or keeping his family safe and dry. He begrudgingly nodded his head and handed the money over for the ponchos. When we got back to our seats he said to the family, "I hope y'all are happy." My mother looked in awe as she couldn't believe what he had sacrificed in buying these bright white ponchos with blue lettering. As we were unpacking the rain gear, a bright smile came across my father's face and he announced, "We can wear them inside out!" So there we sat throughout the game with our ponchos worn wrong side out.

Kentucky proved to be a formidable opponent that day. The Wildcats actually had the lead late in the game until Vince Sutton made a huge throw to Gene Newberry for an Alabama touchdown. Alabama held on to win 31-27. Our long journey was rewarded with a Crimson Tide victory.

As we left the stadium, my father headed to the first large trash can. He started removing the enemy poncho and nodded for us to do the same. One by one, we stuffed this wet plastic into the trash. It was still raining, but I think my father was afraid that we would be seen by some Alabama fan we knew. We walked briskly through the rain on our way back to the car.

Later that night we stopped for dinner. My father was greeted by a stranger who gave him a big "Roll Tide." After speaking with this man for a few minutes, my dad asked my mother to go out to the car. When she returned we wondered why they were giving this man our prized Alabama shakers. When my father rejoined the rest of us, he explained that this man was a big Alabama fan, but he lived in Kentucky. As we had also learned, Alabama gear was not easy to come by in that part of the world so he wanted him to have something.

After dinner, we headed back to Birmingham. I don't remember much of the drive as the events of the day had drained me. When we made it back to the house, I remember my parents carrying us to bed, tucking us in and my father whispering "Roll Tide." We awoke bright and early for church the next morning, all in good spirits because the Lawson family had celebrated another wonderful weekend and an Alabama victory.

Kristi Lawson '00
Birmingham, Alabama

Brian Limbaugh, Chad Hopper, Damon McDonald and Kevin Green

*"Since my head was buried in my hands and everyone around me was still standing, I never saw the flag - offsides Florida and another chance for victory. As the second kick went up, from our vantage point, it too looked wide. I dropped to my seat for the second time all afternoon, certain that another PAT had been blown; however, the deafening roar and the jumping from the Bama fans around me told me that I was wrong."*

*– Chad Hopper*

# OVERTIME REBIRTH
Alabama vs. Florida
October 2, 1999
Florida Field at Ben Hill Griffin Stadium

During my last year at the Capstone, I made the decision to attend as many road football games as I could possibly afford. With or without tickets, I decided to travel to Gainesville, Florida, in 1999 with my friends Brian Limbaugh, Glenn Glover and David Killian. Fresh off a home loss to Louisiana Tech, most Bama fans were not very optimistic. ESPN was already reporting that Alabama could make a coaching change before the '99 season ended.

The Swamp was hot and sticky, even though it was October. The University of Florida, like many schools do now, split their visiting fans in an effort to keep down opposing crowd noise. We were fortunate enough to find tickets in the Alabama section five rows from the field on the 40-yard line. The seats at Florida Field were so close to the sidelines that the players could actually hear what the fans were screaming. That fact also explains why the stadium seems so loud at times.

Florida hit the first big play of the game on a long Doug Johnson touchdown pass. The Tide would answer every Florida score. Later in the first half, Andrew Zow hit a streaking Shaun Alexander releasing out of the backfield for a touchdown – a staple of the 1999 offense. Zow played the game of his career, hitting Antonio Carter for several key third down conversions. However, the momentum of the game was swinging toward the Gators until they fumbled a Bama punt late in the fourth quarter.

Alabama recovered the punt in Florida territory but had to get into the end zone to force overtime. On fourth and short with everyone in the stadium and everyone watching on CBS knowing who was about to get the ball, Alexander burst through the middle for the score. Shaun was a workhorse all season for the Tide, and the fact that he was not in New York for the '99 Heisman ceremony was a travesty.

At the end of regulation, the #2 nationally ranked Gators and Bama were tied at 33. After Florida scored on a pass play in overtime and missed the point after, Alexander followed the block of Chris Samuels for a 25-yard jaunt. The extra point would give Bama a major upset.

It was no good.

I dropped to my seat for the first time all afternoon. I was literally sick to my stomach. We had traveled so far, and the team had played too hard to lose. The already obnoxious Gator fans were really going to be terrible after this game. What were the chances that both Florida and Alabama would miss extra points in overtime on consecutive possessions? Since my head was buried in my hands and everyone around me was still standing, I never saw the flag - offsides Florida and another chance for victory. As the second kick went up it too looked wide from our vantage point. I dropped to my seat for the second time all afternoon, certain that another PAT had been blown; however, the deafening roar and the jumping from the Bama fans around me told me I was wrong.

IT WAS GOOD!

At that moment, I did not know I was watching the 1999 SEC Champions. I did not know that this team would later become the first Crimson Tide team to win at Auburn, but I did know that I was one of the luckiest and happiest people in America on that hot October day in Gainesville.

Chad A. Hopper '00
Centre, Alabama

Legion Field

*"There was a definite mixture of emotions.
On the one hand, we had just come from
behind to beat Auburn, and on the other, we
were losing a great coach and an even better
person – a man who had for seven seasons been
a wonderful ambassador for The University,
leading us to our 12th National Championship
and restoring the pride and swagger that had
been missing since the days of Coach Bryant."*

*– Damon McDonald*

# A DATE TO REMEMBER

Growing up in Alabama, college football is king. At birth, you choose sides. You are either a Tiger or a Tider, and in my case, I bleed crimson and white. For that reason, November 23, 1996 is a date I will remember for the rest of my life. It was a day filled with great emotion – my first time to witness the Iron Bowl in person. One minute I was on an unbelievable high and the next a stunning low. The Iron Bowl always brings that out, but for this one, the mood was intensified because I was there.

That November evening at Legion Field was everything I dreamed of as a child. All day long I couldn't wait for the game to begin. The atmosphere was unlike any other game I had been to as a Bama fan. It was like you could hear everybody's heart beat around you. Being in the company of close friends, everything was set for a great night.

It started as a fantastic evening. Bama jumped out to 17-0 lead, and the crowd was going crazy. It was truly electric and everything I had always wanted to experience. Watching on television or listening to the radio does not do justice to seeing and hearing the roar of an Iron Bowl crowd. And since it was after the days of the split stadium, the sound after a Bama score was especially deafening. Unfortunately, silence soon fell upon Legion Field as Auburn rallied to take a 23-17 lead by halftime.

During the third quarter and most of the fourth, neither team scored. I could not believe that my first Iron Bowl would end like this. However, with just under two minutes to go, Alabama quarterback Freddie Kitchens began to redeem his previous mistakes, and with precious few seconds remaining, he found an open Dennis Riddle on a swing pass, ending a beautiful 80 yard drive with a touchdown, and the score was tied. The extra point split the uprights, giving Bama the lead and a 24-23 win. The pure joy of that moment is priceless to a lifetime Crimson Tide follower. The cups, coke, ice and who knows what else flying through the air as Riddle scored could not have made me any happier. Complete strangers were hugging, people were crying, and the stadium was swaying back and forth. It was simply amazing.

I felt as if nothing could bring me down from that moment of ecstasy, but something did just that. Outside the stadium people were soon gathered around TVs and radios listening to Coach Gene Stallings announce his retirement. There was a definite mixture of emotions. On the one hand, we had just come from behind to beat Auburn, and on the other, we were losing a great coach and an even better person – a man who had for seven seasons been a wonderful ambassador for The University, leading us to our 12th National Championship and restoring the pride and swagger that had been missing since the days of Coach Bryant. To say the least, November 23, 1996, was a bittersweet night – a Daniel Moore moment, then a huge let down, and my first Iron Bowl to see in person - a date to always remember.

Damon McDonald
Piedmont, Alabama

Photo submitted by Linda Huffman

Dwight Stephenson, Linda Huffman, Shaud Williams and
Bob Baumhower

Don Stowe, Joey Stowe and Paul Bryant, Jr.

*"For the past 15 years on the day of the first Tuscaloosa game, there is also another tradition we continue to observe – the Bryant Namesake Reunion. It never ceases to amaze me the number of people who have also paid tribute to Coach Bryant by naming their children after him."*

*– Don Stowe*

— 𝒜 —

# NAMESAKES AND NEW ORLEANS ALABAMA LEGACIES

When my son was born, my wife, Geraldine and I thought long and hard about what name to bestow on our new arrival. Of course, he would have the family last name to someday pass to future generations and since we are an Alabama family and lifelong admirers of Coach Paul Bryant, we decided to pay tribute to the greatest coach to ever live by using the name "Bryant" for our son's middle name. So, Joseph Bryant Stowe arrived already destined for a life filled with crimson and white.

I have always taken Geraldine, my daughter, Allison, and Joey to Bama games in the fall. As the years go by and my children get older, this is one tradition that remains intact. For the past 15 years on the day of the first Tuscaloosa game, there is also another tradition we continue to observe – the Bryant Namesake Reunion. It never ceases to amaze me the number of people who have also paid tribute to Coach Bryant by naming their children after him. Given the countless ways Coach Bryant and his family impacted and continue to impact our community and state, I cannot think of a better way for people to express their deep gratitude. Not surprisingly, the reunion becomes larger each fall.

I have always enjoyed being associated with a champion, and The University of Alabama has always consisted of just that

– champions. I had the honor of personally witnessing my first national championship, and Alabama's twelfth, in January 1993 when a friend of mine and I caught a train bound for the Crescent City. We boarded the Amtrak in Anniston, Alabama anticipating the Tide's long-awaited contest against the #1 ranked Miami Hurricanes. As the train rolled toward the Superdome, it made countless stops where the Alabama faithful on board welcomed more supporters by chanting "Roll Tide." I'm sure that trains have a maximum capacity but seriously doubt it was observed on this journey, and as the train became more full and even somewhat uncomfortable, there was not a single person on board who cared. To the contrary, the more the merrier, as we were all on the same team.

After seven hours, we finally arrived at our destination. Being that kickoff was over a day away, we enjoyed the sights and sounds of New Orleans while gathering our thoughts about the upcoming showdown with the 'Canes. During this time, I cannot begin to tell you how obnoxious the Miami fans were, shouting all types of obscenities at every Alabama fan they could find. It was also during this time that I have never been prouder to be for the Tide as I never observed any Bama supporter dignify the insults with a response. We all thought – just wait until game time and we'll see who the real champions are.

We did just that. Gino Torretta never knew what hit him. He was simply a deer caught in headlights all night long as Brother Oliver's defense pounded him into the turf, and when he was not lying flat on his back, he was chasing George Teague and other Bama defenders who intercepted several of his passes.

And speaking of big plays, I was seated on the 30-yard line where the greatest play in history took place. Just when the

Allison and Joey Stowe with Big Al

Miami receiver caught what should have easily been a long touchdown pass and was literally 15 yards ahead of the closest Tide defender, George Teague amazingly came out of nowhere and caught the receiver from behind. It gets better. Before I could come to grips with what I had just seen, I suddenly saw that Teague had the ball and was headed the other way. And to think that this all happened right in front of me! At that time, I just hoped that the cameraman caught all of this so I could watch it later and maybe one day believe what I had just seen.

The rest is well-known history – 34-13. And speaking of Miami fans, there weren't any left around after the game. They were all headed back to South Florida, and we were about to enjoy a celebration reserved for champions – National Champions. I arrived back at the hotel around 3 a.m., and the train was to depart three hours later. I barely slept a wink because I was so excited about the game and proud for The University – not a bad way to welcome the New Year.

As time goes by, I often reflect on the '93 Sugar Bowl and the way Alabama fans, coaches, and players responded when faced with what the media called insurmountable odds. Though Coach Bryant's reign was several years passed, the dignity, tradition, and class that he brought to Alabama football was still alive. We were indeed National Champions.

Don Stowe
Centre, Alabama

Jack LeCroy, Joey Stowe and Danny LeCroy

Jarrod Bazemore and his family at graduation in '95

*"...I have discovered that something magical happens when people write about a topic close to their hearts. They give you more than just a story on paper – they give you a piece of their lives."*

*– Jarrod Bazemore*

# MORE TO COME. . .

When approached by my brother-in-law, Clint Lovette, about co-authoring this book, I confess that while flattered, I was also reluctant. My weeks and often time weekends are filled with the demands of my profession, and I haven't a wealth of spare time to say the least.

During those rare occasions when I'm not working, I try to devote my time to my wife, Holly, and our 17 month old son, Jackson, and occasionally, I pursue my beloved hobby of flying. So, why did I decide to jump aboard Tales of the Tide? The answer is simple. As best put by Coach Bryant, "Mama called."

I met my wife and some of my closest friends at The University and grew even closer to many of my hometown friends during my time there, all while obtaining an invaluable education without which I would not be where I am today. Put simply, it was seven of the best years of my life. That's why.

During my work on this book, I have had the opportunity of rekindling old friendships and making new ones, all while having the honor of hearing what our state school means to so many of you. I have been able to work with a great publisher and help compile a work which I hope will be read by the masses and passed on through generations to come. True, The University of Alabama's rich tradition was built on victories and championships won on the field, but the perpetuity of this tradition is dependent on the memories and stories from you and me – the fans.

To all of those who submitted stories and photographs for this book, I thank you; however, I would be remiss if I didn't note that obtaining these stories in written form was not as simple as I first thought. The art of writing is not easy, and many are often times hesitant to reduce their inner-most thoughts to manuscript- me included.

Despite this natural reluctance, the stories we received were excellent. Through my experience with this book, I have discovered that something magical happens when people write about a topic close to their hearts. They give you more than just a story on paper – they give you a piece of their lives. And it's damn good.

As you have probably already discovered, this book offers a wide variety of stories. There are stories of buzzer beaters, walk-off homeruns, victories over Auburn, championships, marriages, and even mamas and papas. Some are very humorous, practically leaving you in tears from laughter. Others bring tears of another kind, most likely akin to the deep feelings and love you harbor for our school, and when you put them all together, it's easy to see why The University of Alabama is second to none.

To all reading this book, I offer you my deep gratitude and greatly look forward to hopefully meeting you in the near future. If you by chance ever recognize me in public, I hope you will take the time to say "hello" so we can discuss what The University means to you, and if you are ever having difficulty finding someone with whom to discuss the Tide, give me a call – I'm in the book. There's nothing I enjoy more than reliving old Alabama victories and talking about the many to come, and now that I've had my first taste of authorship with this book, I turn my sights toward its sequel. I certainly pray that Tales of the Tide I finds you well, and rest assured, there's more to come. . .

Won't you join us?

Jarrod Braxton Bazemore '95 & '98
Birmingham, Alabama

Jarrod, Jackson and Holly Bazemore

Clint and Anne Lovette

# ABOUT THE AUTHOR

Lovette & Bazemore, LLC
Members:

Jarrod Braxton Bazemore grew up in Centre, Alabama, graduating as Valedictorian from Cherokee County High School in 1991. He then attended the University of Alabama where he graduated summa cum laude in 1995 with a major in finance and a minor in Spanish and was a member of Pi Kappa Phi Fraternity. During his undergraduate studies, Jarrod achieved membership in Alpha Lambda Delta, Phi Kappa Phi, Beta Gamma Sigma, and Omicron Delta Kappa honor societies, was a two year First Alabama Bank Right Way Scholar, and was awarded the 1995 Alabama Bankers' Association Student Achievement Award. Jarrod graduated from the University of Alabama School of Law (J.D.) in 1998, where he was a three year recipient of the Hugh Reed, Jr., Memorial Scholarship, was a member of Alabama Law & Psychology Review and Bench & Bar Legal Honor Society, and sat for two years as Associate Justice on the University of Alabama School of Law Honor Court. Jarrod practices in Birmingham, Alabama, with the law firm of Spain & Gillon, LLC, and is married to the former Holly Hendrickson of Vestavia Hills, Alabama. The couple has one son, Jackson, and they are members of Canterbury United Methodist Church.

Clint Austin Lovette was born in Birmingham, Alabama and attended Vestavia Hills High School where he played baseball, football and basketball and was a member of the 1992 State Championship and 1993 State runner-up baseball teams. He attended the University of Alabama where he graduated with a degree in Business Management in 1998. He married his high school sweetheart, Anne Hendrickson, in 1998 and they have lived in Birmingham, Alabama since graduation from The Capstone. He has spent the last 9 years in business development and is currently the National Sales Manager for the Web Technologies division of SunGard.

# A SPECIAL THANK YOU
# FROM THE PUBLISHER

Thank you for buying Tales of the Tide.© We sincerely hope that you have enjoyed reading these stories and sharing a few of the moments that make up a portion of the storied Crimson Tradition. FANtastic Memories offers our gratitude to the individuals and organizations that contributed to the development and production of this book, making this concept a reality.

We want to thank the true champions of this book, Clint Lovette and Jarrod Bazemore of Lovette & Bazemore, LLC who assisted in writing, collecting, editing, and compiling the wonderful stories that you have read. These University of Alabama Alumni represent the greatness of the Alabama Tradition, and their love for their University is revealed in their efforts to complete this work.

FANtastic Memories would also like to thank those who assisted our production of Tales of the Tide.© Atticus Communication assisted in providing their expertise in graphic design, layout, and production. Carol Muse Evans contributed with editing, creative content, and proofreading. We would also like to thank Al Blanton for his writing and promotional contributions to this effort.

We appreciate the businesses and individuals that have materially supported our infant company, FANtastic Memories, LLC. Their generous support made this book financially feasible. We have listed these special contributors at the conclusion of the book and on our website www.TalesoftheTide.com. Please support these businesses, as they have supported our effort.

We are also thankful for the true inspiration behind this book, The University of Alabama. This great institution is as one author described, "The Tide That Binds" the Alabama family. We appreciate The University officials who have offered their assistance in bringing this book to you.

We thank our respective family and friends, who have offered tremendous support to our dream of developing this concept. Since this long journey of creating FANtastic Memories, LLC began in April of 2001, our friends and family have sacrificed a great deal of quality time as we planned and prepared. We are thankful that they believe in this concept as much as we do.

# TALES OF THE TIDE©
# SUPPORTERS

This book was created with the goal of celebrating and sharing great stories with Alabama fans everywhere. The authors and FANtastic Memories, LLC have worked tirelessly to create Tales of the Tide© Realizing that we were operating on limited resources, we proceeded with faith that Tales of the Tide© would create a movement that others would appreciate and support.

Indeed, the authors and FANtastic Memories, LLC have received the very generous support of businesses and individuals, making our dream attainable. We are very appreciative of these supporters who believed in Tales of the Tide© and this effort. In turn, we hope that you will take the opportunity to thank the businesses listed on the next few pages and support them with your patronage.

EXERCISE
BUILDS
CHAMPIONS

**Bama All-Time Great Lee Roy Jordan with his grand-children, enjoying Rainbow Play Equipment, designed for the best kids in the world. YOURS.**

*"Your children deserve the best. Let us show you how easy it is to put one in your back yard."*
— Lee Roy Jordan, Owner

We accept major credit cards. Financing available.
Convenient locations throughout Alabama.
Call 1-800-724-6269 for the location nearest you.

**JORDAN RAINBOW PLAY SYSTEMS**

# @tticus

A full-service design firm producing advertising and marketing that sells, for the past 49 years*.

*Good Boy, Atticus!*

*That's 7 years for humans.

atticusweb.com · 205.942.8030 · info@atticusweb.com

*Protect the lives you love*™

Tackling your financial goals doesn't have to be a struggle. Give Protective a call, and we will put you in touch with a financial services coach who will help you call the shots.

For information, please contact:

**Alan E. Watson, CLU, ChFC**
Senior Vice President,
Life and Annuity Division

**205-268-3918**

**Protective** ▲▲▲.
Life Insurance Company
*Doing the right thing is smart business.*™
PLC.1422.08.04

# Unique and Hip
## *Beats*
## predictable and stale
# *Every Time.*

*Event planning isn't about searching for hotel
ballrooms and country clubs anymore.
Enjoy your next affair in the historic and
comfortable atmosphere of the B&A Warehouse,
a venue versatile enough to handle functions from
15 to 1500. Ask us about off premise catering.*

Corporate Functions • Meetings
Parties • Seminars • Exhibitions
Weddings  Birthdays • Formals
Bar Mitzvahs • Bat Mitzvahs

1531 1st Avenue South
Birmingham's Historic
Warehouse District
205.326.4220
www.bawarehouse.com

To some, a typical college football game is limited to a three-hour span on a Saturday afternoon. But in the SEC, fans take it a little more seriously than that. Football isn't just a single game on a specific day—it's a comprehensive experience that spans a full 11 weeks and, very often, beyond. It's built around a long-term commitment with friends and family all coming together and sharing a common bond. At Tiffin Motorhomes, we view our relationships with our customers the same way. Going over and above just making the sale, we strive to form a lasting friendship with every owner. Some people might say that we take it too seriously. But down here, we know everybody understands.

ONLY 144 HOURS UNTIL KICKOFF (We Understand).

www.tiffinmotorhomes.com
256.356.8661

TIFFIN MOTORHOMES
WHEREVER YOU GO, WE GO.

We know that more often than not
it is better to understand than
to be understood.

**ALIANT** BANK
*We know.*

ALEXANDER CITY · BIRMINGHAM · DADEVILLE
MILLBROOK · MONTGOMERY · WETUMPKA

Member FDIC

# A Good Insurance Company Is Always On The Ball.

PEANUTS © United Feature Syndicate, Inc., www.snoopy.com

At MetLife we'll rush to your service and tackle your insurance and other financial needs. Don't fumble around with anyone else.

**Terry Bagwell**
**3800 Colonnade Parkway Suite 600**
**Birmingham, AL 35243**
**205-970-9782 X 105**

**have you met life today?**ˢᵐ

# MetLife® Financial Services

A division of
Metropolitan Life Insurance Company, New York, NY
9409A67-MLIC-LD

### Manufacturers Represented

ACRA Machine Tools
Action Superabrasives
Advent Thread Mills
All-American Drill Bushing
Allied Machine & Eng
Allison Abrasives
American Buff Intl
American Drill Bushings
Amplex Superabrasives
Arc Abrasives
Armstrong Blum Mfg
Bay State / Tyrolit
Brown & Sharpe
Brubaker Tool
Carborundum
Carr Lane Mfg
CGS Tool
Circle Cutting Tools
Circle Machine
CJT / Koolcarb
Collis
Command Corp
Corman Supplies
Craig Tools
Criterion Machine
DeWalt Power Tools
Desmond-Stephan Mfg.
Dihart
Dijet of America
Dorian Tool
Dormer Tool
Duramet
Fette
Fullerton Tool
Future Abrasives

Graymills Pumps
Guhring
Hangsterfer's Labs
Hanita
Hannibal Carbide
Hoosier Broach
Ingersoll Cutting Tool Co
J & M Diamond
Jacobs Chuck Mfg. Co.
Jancy Engineering
Jergens
Johnson Carbide
Kennametal
Keo Cutter
Knight Carbide
Komet of America
Lavallee & Ide
Lexington Cutter
Liberty Special Tool
L.S. Starrett
M A Ford
Markal Products
Marvel
Melcut
Merit Abrasives
Metcut
Michigan Drill
Modern Abrasives
Moon Cutter
Nachi America
Nachi Machining
New England Tap Corp.
Niagara Cutter
Nikken USA
North American Tool

Norton
NTK
OSG/Sossner
Parlec
PH Horn
Quality Carbide
Quality Chaser
Kennametal
Regal Cutting Tools
Rego-Fix
Riten Centers
Royal Products
RTW
Scully Jones
SGS Tool
Southern Gage
Spartan Ironwkrs
SPI
Sticks & Stones
Suburban Tool
Tap Magic
Techleader
Thurston
Tool Flo Mfg
Toshiba Tungaloy
TSD-Univeral
Tyrolit Abrasives
United Drill Bushing
Universal Toolholdg
Valenite Valcool
Vermont Gage
Vermont Tap & Die
Widell
Wright Tool
YMW Tap & Die

| MaxTool, Inc. Birmingham | MaxTool, Inc. Huntsville | MaxTool, Inc. Montgomery |
|---|---|---|
| 119-B Citation Court | 2025 Sparkman Drive | 411-A #2 Twain Curve |
| Birmingham, AL 35209 | Huntsville, AL 35810 | Montgomery, AL 36107 |
| phone: 205.942.2466 | phone: 256.859.3100 | phone: 334.279.6113 |
| fax: 205.942.7144 | fax: 256.851.6803 | fax: 334.279.7470 |

**Owner: Dudley Barton**
**University of Alabama Class of '72**

# Collegiate Event Services, Inc.

*Contact us for all your t-shirt design and printing needs.*

Phone: (205)620-5322
Fax: (205)620-5313
Email: sales@tshirtfever.com

P.O. Box 36202
Birmingham AL 35236

**Website: www.tshirtfever.com**

# IT'S NOT JUST COOLING
## IT'S THE WINNING EDGE.

*Port-A-Cool® portable evaporative cooling units cool hot athletes on the sidelines so they are refreshed, energized and ready to get back in the game.*

**AS SEEN ON NFL SIDELINES!**

U.S. Patent 6,502,414
U.S. Patent 6,233,548
U.S. Patent D 382905

*"The Port-A-Cool® system from General Shelters has definitely been a factor in the success of the 1992 Dallas Cowboys. There are many different types of fans available, but the Port-A-Cool® system actually cools the air on our sidelines. I couldn't be more pleased with this product and I recommend it highly."*

Kevin O'Neill - Head Athletic Trainer for the Dallas Cowboys

- Patented evaporative cooling technology
- Lowers temperature of ambient air an average of 20° F.
- Operates efficiently with only 110 volt power source and tap water
- Simple maintenance and operation and long-term dependability
- Four fan sizes: 48", 36", 24", and 16"
- Meets cooling needs in a variety of applications ... anywhere traditional air-conditioning is impractical or unavailable.

*Port-A-Cool® units are manufactured by General Shelters of Texas S.B., Ltd.*
*Center, Texas • www.port-a-cool.com*
ph **800-695-2942** • fx **936-598-8901**

Located in Montgomery's Mulberry District,
our shop is easy to find. We are on the corner
of Mulberry Street and West Fifth Street.

1834 West Fifth Street
Montgomery, Alabama 36106

Call us! 334.356.2933
Email: wedsbyjill@yahoo.com
Web: www.weddingsbyjill.com
Fax: 334.356.2932

# MODULAR CONNECTIONS, LLC

*Connecting you to the best building solutions*

Modular Connections is a premier supplier of factory
built buildings, shelters, and equipment enclosures.

**Some of the markets we serve:**

| | |
|---|---|
| *Telecommunications* | *Homeland Security* |
| *Electric Utility* | *Military Applications* |
| *Water Utility* | *Commercial Structures* |
| *School Classrooms* | *Retail Kiosks* |

**Contact Us:**

Phone: 205.980.4565  sales@ModularConnections.com
Fax: 800-856-4666  www.ModularConnections.com

**The Premiere Parenting Resource for the Birmingham Community**

**www.BirminghamParent.com**

**Reaching 80,000 readers and growing!**

For locations on where to pick up your free copy today, please contact us.

**205-663-5070**

imagine what's in store

| **Peggy's Hallmark** | **Peggy's Hallmark** |
| --- | --- |
| 1550 Montgomery Hwy | 1054 Main Street |
| Hoover, AL 35216 | Gardendale, AL 35071 |
| (205) 979-1477 | (205) 631-0055 |

*Stop by and pick up a copy of Tales of the Tide* ©
*as a gift for your favorite Alabama fan.*

When you care enough to send the very best

**PHOTO FINISH**

*Where Tide fans take their film.*

**25% off if you mention**
**Tales of the Tide** [©]

2409 Acton Road ▪ Vestavia, Alabama 35243

   205.824.7848

**1 Hour or Next Day Service**
*E-6 ▪ Black & White ▪ Enlargements*
*Corporate Accounts Welcome*

*10% off Gameday & Tailgating pictures*

---

LEE PRESSURE WASHING
Residential/Commercial
Phone: 205.296.4338
Nextel: 102381 *1

# TALES OF THE TIDE SUPPORTERS

Tommy and Stephanie Atkinson

Dixon and Camille Barth

John and Kim Barth

Dudley Barton

Richard and Linda Benson

Jerry and Sarah Bentley

Sandy Bills

Terry and Linda Birchfield

Laura Blake

Bobby and Sandra Bracknell

Tim and Kim Brannon

Eric Caldwell

Bobby Cook

David and Vicki Denmark

Jay and Linda Donaldson

Cade and Allison Festavan

Kevin and Wendy Festavan

Randy and Deidre Festavan

Kent Gidley

Tommy and Carol Godwin

Jay Green

Danny and Pam Griffin

"Wild Bill Handley"

Marland and Denise Hayes

Cliff and Lisa Hembree

Hong Kong Tailors

Bob and Linda Huffman

Kevin Kilgore

The Kirkland Family

Joe and Suzy Koski

Matt Koski

Randy Lambert

Ken Land

Dennis Ledbetter

Len and Margaret Lee

Susan McElroy

Mitchell and Dana Moss

Rick and Sandy Pickering

Kevin Renzetti

Tim Renzetti

Brian and Robin Russell

Julie Rynearson

Chris and Branda Stovall

Tim Street

Rusty and Lisa Thomas

Lynn Thrash

Phil and Jenny Thrasher

Robert and Emma Aycock

Jim Webb

Jeff Wisner

Cameron Yager

Daryl and Nicole Yager

Gavin Yager

# AUTHOR INDEX

| Author | Page(s) | Author | Page(s) |
|---|---|---|---|
| Ayers, I. Daniel | 83 | Lee, Lindsay | 107 |
| Ballard, Vance | 149 | Limbaugh, Brian | 89, 191 |
| Basgier, Summer | 203 | Lovette, Clint | 1, 37 |
| Bazemore, Jarrod | 25, 253 | Lovette, Jim | 97 |
| Black, Amanda | 165 | Martin, Andy | 93 |
| Blanton, Al | 121, 227 | Massey, Rayford | 119 |
| Brandino, Tony | 21, 163 | Massey, Julie | 187 |
| Birchfield, Linda | 219 | McDonald, Damon | 243 |
| Cahalan, Kyle | 125 | Middlebrooks, Vicki | 223, 225 |
| Campbell, Joey | 197 | Mize, Scott | 71 |
| Curry, Stuart | 155 | Moore, Kelly | 213 |
| Dease, Ernie | 174 | Morano, Spence | 129 |
| Duncan, Barney | 103 | Murray, David | 230 |
| Evans, Heidi | 199 | Olivet, David | 67 |
| Ford, Brenda | 195 | Pickering, Brad | 145 |
| Foster, Greg | 153 | Proctor, Michelle | 29 |
| Gidley, James | 43 | Roberson, James | 111 |
| Jordan, Lee Roy | vii | Shannon, Kylie | 133 |
| Hampton, Chris | 63 | Sloan, Steve | 17 |
| Harper, Jennifer | 49 | Stanfield, Elise | 137 |
| Hendrickson, Robert | 171 | Stephens, Daphne | 167 |
| Hill, Mary | 211 | Stewart, Jr., Charles | 177 |
| Hopper, Chad | 7, 239 | Stowe, Don | 247 |
| Huffman, Mark | 159 | Stutts, Eugene | 115 |
| Kennedy, Mike | 53 | Tiffin, Bob | 11 |
| Lawson, Paul | 207 | Tombrello, Joseph | 77 |
| Lawson, Kristi | 233 | Turner, Kevin | 80 |
| Lee, Len | 59 | | |

# FUTURE BOOK INFORMATION

We Sincerely Hope That You Have Enjoyed Reading

## TALES OF THE TIDE©
"A Book By Alabama Fans… For Alabama Fans"

The 2nd Edition is already underway.

### TELL US WHAT YOU THOUGHT OF THE BOOK

We would like to read your thoughts about the book
so please send us your comments.

### DO YOU HAVE A GREAT
### CRIMSON TIDE MEMORY TO SHARE?

If so, please submit your story or story concept in writing to our website or by mail. If your story is not complete, that's OK. We will assist you in developing your thoughts and in making the perfect Alabama story.

VISIT OUR WEBSITE AT: www.TalesoftheTide.com

E-MAIL YOUR STORY: Info@TalesoftheTide.com

OR

MAIL TO:

Tales of the Tide
P.O. Box 660582
Birmingham, AL 35266

# QUICK ORDER FORM

Email orders: Order@TalesoftheTide.com

Telephone orders: 205-585-1785

Postal orders: Tales of the Tide,
P.O. Box 660582, Birmingham, AL 35266

Website orders: www.TalesoftheTide.com

# TALES OF THE TIDE©

**Number of copies:** _____ @ $19.95 each + $1.60 each (8% Sales Tax if in Alabama)

**Shipping/Handling:** $4 for first book ($2 each additional)

**Total:** _____

Name:_____

Address: _____

City:_____ Zip:_____

Phone: _____

Email Address: _____

**Payment:** ☐ Check  ☐ Visa  ☐ MC  ☐ AmEx  ☐ Discover

Card Number: _____

Name on Card: _____ Exp. date:_____

Personalized Signed Copies (Insert Message):

_____

*Visa, MasterCard, Discover, AMEX Accepted Online www.TalesoftheTide.com*